THE

QUARTERLY

EDITED BY

GORDON LISH

THE
QUARTERLY

6 / SUMMER 1988

VINTAGE BOOKS

A DIVISION OF RANDOM HOUSE

NEW YORK

THE QUARTERLY (ISSN 0893-3103) IS EDITED BY GORDON LISH
AND IS PUBLISHED MARCH, JUNE, SEPTEMBER, AND DECEMBER
FOR $28 THE YEAR ($42 IN CANADA) BY VINTAGE BOOKS,
A DIVISION OF RANDOM HOUSE, INC., 201 EAST 50TH STREET,
NEW YORK, NY 10022. APPLICATION TO MAIL AT SECOND-CLASS
POSTAGE RATES IS PENDING AT NEW YORK, NY, AND
AT ADDITIONAL MAILING OFFICES. SEND ORDERS AND ADDRESS
CHANGES TO THE QUARTERLY, SUBSCRIPTION DEPARTMENT,
VINTAGE BOOKS, FIFTEENTH FLOOR, 201 EAST 50TH STREET,
NEW YORK, NY 10022.
THE QUARTERLY WELCOMES THE OPPORTUNITY TO READ WORK
OF EVERY CHARACTER, AND IS ESPECIALLY CONCERNED
TO KEEP ITSELF AN OPEN FORUM. MANUSCRIPTS
MUST BE ACCOMPANIED BY THE CUSTOMARY RETURN MATERIALS,
AND SHOULD BE ADDRESSED TO THE EDITOR, THE QUARTERLY,
201 EAST 50TH STREET, NEW YORK, NY 10022. THE QUARTERLY
MAKES THE UTMOST EFFORT TO OFFER ITS RESPONSE TO
MANUSCRIPTS NO LATER THAN ONE WEEK SUBSEQUENT
TO RECEIPT. OPINIONS EXPRESSED HEREIN ARE NOT NECESSARILY
THOSE OF THE EDITOR OR OF THE PUBLISHER.

ISBN: 0-394-75719-X

DESIGN BY ANDREW ROBERTS
MANAGEMENT BY DENISE STEWART AND ELLEN F. TORRON

MANUFACTURED IN THE UNITED STATES OF AMERICA

THE QUARTERLY HAS BEEN TURNING UP NO FEW COMMENDATIONS FOR
THE QUALITY OF ITS APPEARANCE. RATHER CONSIDERABLE ATTENTION HAS
BEEN PAID MOST PARTICULARLY TO THE RENDERING OF OUR COVERS,
VARIATIONS ON A THEME AS EXECUTED BY LORRAINE LOUIE. THOUGH WE
HAVE NOT REMARKED EACH CITATION MS. LOUIE HAS WON FOR THE
QUARTERLY, THE TYPE DIRECTORS AWARD FOR EXCELLENCE IN DESIGN
SEEMS TOO SIGNIFICANT AN ACHIEVEMENT FOR THE EDITOR TO FAIL TO
CONGRATULATE MS. LOUIE AND TO THANK HER, AS PUBLICLY AS MIGHT
BE MANAGED, FOR HER BRINGING SUCH AN HONOR TO US. THIS ALSO
SEEMS A FINE TIME FOR THE EDITOR TO MAKE A STATEMENT OF HIS
GRATITUDE TO CERTAIN PERSONS WHOSE LABORS THIS MAGAZINE SO
ENTIRELY RELIES ON—NAMELY, VICTORIA MATHEWS, LINDA ROSENBERG,
TASHA HALL, SUSAN MITCHELL, AND IRENA VUKOV-KENDES.

THE
QUARTERLY

still no Trail

Switzerland

Romantic, of course, had been the first word she'd thought of, it coming to her right in the middle of the Atlantic Ocean. Except that what it left out about Switzerland—*Switzerland is romantic*—was all the neat and tidy part. The little round-ish man, for instance, the one in the gray suit across the aisle. Or the map up on the screen in front with its nifty little replica of their airplane, which sort of twitched ahead of itself every one hundred and twenty seconds. Or that cute little mini-bottle of wine that came automatically with the meal, of that delicious wine with the tiny bubbles in it, that wine the name of which she had better be putting in her little notebook—her little notebook with all the little clocks on the cover. And even the smoked eel, it looked as if she could have eaten it if she'd had to, it being more like a little rectangle than a snake. Well, perhaps not a rectangle but a trapezoid, at any rate. And about that size too, about the size of a trapezoid in a math book, if you could pardon her using an expression which showed that what she hadn't yet done—even after nearly thirty-five hundred miles—was too much branching out.

Although maybe she would.

Because now she was feeling just as light and feathery as one of those clouds puffed up under her. And even if the headrest she'd just relaxed back on didn't exactly feel as if it were one of those clouds, it certainly was as neat and tidy as she could have hoped.

Although, in spite of those little clouds and also the clouds on the postcard, the clouds with the mountain peaks coming up through them, what she wasn't back to considering—even after all this thinking about clouds—was the word *cloud-filled.* Because if you bothered to consider all that they had done for her—not just the school but that generous Mr. Garfield whom she hadn't yet had the pleasure of meeting, that generous new parent, Mr. Garfield, who had arranged not just for the hotel on the little river but also for the suite, for the suite for the price of a room—she couldn't use the word *cloud-filled*.

Well, she didn't know what the right word was, but the plane was feeling as if it was coming down, which a glance at her wristwatch confirmed. Confirmed that they were about to head down into the clouds. Those white, fluffy clouds that looked soft enough to sleep on.

Which, if it didn't sound so intimate—*soft enough to sleep on*—might have been, as an opener for describing Switzerland, quite a good one.

Well, she must say, she was thinking, sitting with her two bags right by her side for easy exit from this modern subway; well, she must say, there was no question about it, that the modernness of it, of the airport, or the flughafen, or whatever it was called, had surprised her, its signs for where you had to go hanging right down in front of your eyes even if you weren't looking for them, the ceilings were so low. So that even if you tried, you'd have trouble not getting there, to where you were going, those signs were hanging down so low, and it was all so convenient.

Which, now that she was thinking about it, really was quite like Switzerland, its being so organized.

And another thing about the airport that was just nifty was the way the baggage carts went right up the escalators with the people standing right behind them, and as casually as if there were no way in the world that the force of those things could slide back down on top of you.

Which is all she'd been doing—trying to watch the other people getting the knack of it before she tried it for herself—when that nice man, the same man in the gray suit on the plane, had been beckoning her to go on up ahead of him, and so she'd been forced into just relaxing and pretending that it was the most natural thing in the world to edge your baggage cart onto an escalator—as if it were not the edge of an escalator you were getting up to but the edge of something that would drop off into nothing—when, before she knew it, the front wheel really had just hitched on and the whole cart really was just gripping on by itself, hanging there at a forty-five degree angle without slipping back, half on and half off each step, and going up anyway.

As if it were a person going on up before they—before that person, that is—had decided to.

Compared to the flughafen, was how she would begin this section.

Yes, compared to the flughafen this train station was just like the ones in the Impressionist paintings, and just what she'd expected—gray steam hissing from the waiting trains, and the ceiling was gray, too, and vaulted, and ribbed.

Like being in the inside of a huge reptile, almost.

Which was the way, in her little notebook, that she would phrase it.

And at just 8:04 the train took off.

A cute little red train, almost like a toy, with neat little buttonlike things you pulled up and down on to open and close the windows, and little white linen napkins for the headrest on which you could see the snaps—which was reassuring, the way that in a jiffy the dirty napkins could be snapped off and clean ones snapped back on.

And here was a line she liked—*a Swiss train was something to set your watch by.*

Although, now that she was actually thinking about it, the first things they were passing were not at all like Switzerland—little sheds put together with patches of corrugated tin and wood boards, all brownish in color, and in front of each, plots of brownish ground that maybe were cultivated or maybe were not—you couldn't tell, it being winter—and all she could see were clumps of withered plants, a little like the cabbages a bunny might nestle in if they had been green, and in front of some of these plots were gnarled branches, which, if they weren't dead, were dormant; all of which, these plots of brownish ground and dilapidated huts, which, even if in a few months would be covered up again in leaves or in foliage—in *foliage like feathers,* being a good way of saying it—was still not how she pictured Switzerland, except for the way they came one after the other, say, as the lines on a clock did, did come one after the other.

Although, as far as the people on the train, they did look like Switzerland, like a container full of Switzerland, especially one, the man she had seen on the plane, a man whom you could concentrate on as being the most Swiss of all, a roundish sort of man in a neat gray business suit—even though what he was wearing didn't make him look as if he belonged on a train going up to the mountains, which was probably because in another stop or two, at some well-organized, small Swiss business city, he'd be getting off; a man who looked the most like Switzerland not just for his roundish figure, his cushiony form that looked as if it had been stuffed with something that was maybe as dense as goose liver, but even more for his mustache, now that she'd had time to look up at it more closely while he wasn't watching, his mustache that looked just like a toothbrush, it was so well organized—a twiggy, brownish natural-bristle toothbrush, the kind that she had seen in the airport in the airport pharmacy but which, in her opinion, was probably impractical, the bristles coming right out just as if the animal were shedding, not to mention its being expensive, twenty-seven Swiss francs, or, in dollars—she had her little converter just handily clipped on the band of her watch—nearly eighteen American dollars.

And now they were chugging rhythmically along the side of a huge open lake.

And rising from the lake all along the opposite shore was the base of an upright mountain, which was rising so straight up from the lake it looked like the leg of a person standing up to applaud someone, which was rising so straight up it looked like, now that she thought of it, the base of some huge tree, it was so thick, or better, the leg, and the foot too, of an immense gray mammal, a thick bone running vertically—you could almost see it—beneath the gray skin of the mountain, and at the very bottom, some spots of pure rock where the toenails would be, which were there probably because the vegetation had been rubbed off there, and farther up there were wispy grayish trees that from this distance looked like the faint hairs that, if you thought of it, you can see grouped around here and there on the skins of very old elephants.

Well, she really did feel, as they went along, that she was getting better at it, at this describing.

And now they were in open fields.

And here was a kind of tree she didn't know the name of, but without leaves on it, which looked like an upside-down broom, not an American broom with a long handle, or a feather duster either, but the kind of broom that is made of twigs gathered up at one end, which you can buy in tourist shops, say, at a place like Williamsburg; while all along, as they were getting higher, the plain brown ground, punctual as a clock, was beginning to get white, first in patches, then in larger slabs, until finally, farther up, she could see where it got solid—the whiteness—except for the interception of what she was thinking were the trees, but which looked like nothing that could hold the snow from slipping downward, which looked like nothing—from this distance—more than feathers.

And as the train went higher, not winding its way as she had pictured it would do but going as straight up as, say, the baggage carts had on the escalator, the broom trees disappeared altogether, as if, in the white snow up higher, there wouldn't be anything to need them for—a notion she liked too, especially since it fit so well with her neat and tidy theme; and replacing those broom trees were nondeciduous trees, very tall nondeciduous trees with very black trunks and branches, at least in this early morning light, and very scraggly—scraggly and droopy, as, say, the frame of that poor Ellen Lewis's father underneath his suit, or how she imagined it, anyway, and with wispy little unorganized twigs coming off each branch, and from those wispy little twigs, lots of black things—black things like shriveled fruits—hanging down.

Well, she didn't know how to describe these trees, to describe them in a way that would just pluck them up and onto a postcard the way *brooms* had for the broom trees.

And now here was another kind of tree that was coming up more and more, whose name she didn't know either, and which, even though they were definitely nondeciduous trees and had pine needles, had the kind of color—or noncolor, rather—that made it not quite right to call them *evergreen.*

And another thing she was noticing about Switzerland was that when the cute little train stopped at each of the little gray concrete stations, the young men in uniforms had their jackets a little too short in the back—not that she minded, seeing just that little bit that the jacket should have covered, except that it looked rather awkward, which made her wonder if these jackets were fitted separately, or if they were company clothes, exchanged like the pillow covers on a hotel bed, an observation which was so good that she thought she ought to put it into her little notebook right away—*exchanged their clothes like pillow covers*—her little notebook which, now that she thought about it, had such an appropriate design on it—all sorts of clocks with all the little seconds drawn in on each. All the little pin-size lines that made you so aware of the seconds that they, that the seconds, seemed to be not just ticking but prickling you as they passed.

And then she remembered to enter *fondant,* the word for that bubbly Swiss wine that she liked, not that she usually liked wine.

And also her little code to help her pronounce it. Not *fond ant*—people are fond of ants—because they aren't, was how she would remember that that wasn't the right pronunciation. But *fawn dawn*—dawn being a likely time to see fawns—because that was true, at least as far as she imagined it.

Which made her wonder, as their little train was passing through the woods, if she might not see a deer.

And now in the distance she could see a pure white mountain like a cloud, or like a pillow of clouds, behind the crisscross of two steep slopes.

Although that wasn't the right way of saying it, she knew.

Because that description, the pillow description, made the mountain sound right there, right under your head and very big. Whereas the *mountain like a pillow* was a backdrop far in the distance.

And also because it probably wouldn't look like a pillow at all from close up, or like a cloud either—because of the rocks and trees and things like that that she was sure that you could see up there, coming up from its surface.

And then, suddenly, their little train whooshed into the darkness of a tunnel she hadn't seen coming.

Of a long tunnel—because still they were in it, and because it had no light coming in yet to judge the distance by, just the ticking of the wheels.

Well, speaking of ticking, or time ticking, or of it prickling, rather, one of the things she had to do when she got to the hotel and got settled was to write, not to the trustees—she would do that later—but to that new parent, Mr. Garfield. To write to him, well, to drop him a note, that was a better way of considering it, to drop him a note thanking him, to drop him a note kindly thanking him for arranging—she might as well be getting her wording organized—to thank him for kindly arranging for the room in the hotel, in the nice new hotel that had just been opened in the quaint little Swiss town, the hotel, that is, that perhaps he was a part owner of, or something of the sort—although she wasn't going to refer to anything like that, quite naturally.

And to thank him for requesting not just any room, but a room on the water, a room on the little river, so that she—or, rather, not *she* in particular, but whoever it was who was going to be sent—so that *they,* so that this person, that is, could lie back on their pillow, or on his, or on her pillow, rather—so that this person could lie back watching the geese out on the water, which was one of the hotel specialities—the Ganserhof, the hotel was called, which meant *goose* in German, or in Swiss-German, or in whatever language it was called; and also she had to thank him—she had to fit this in too—for writing to the hotel to say that if one was available, it being perhaps a little after the season, she could also have—she, or that person, rather—for the price of a single room, a suite.

Then, suddenly, or at least so it seemed, so it seemed probably because she had been thinking too much about the phrasing of the note about the suite, and then about the kind of bed they would probably have in a suite, which was seeming a little too much for a person like herself, not only because she didn't travel with so many things that they needed to be spread out, but also because she herself didn't need to spread out too much, sleeping with her arms down at her sides and her legs together, her whole body not branched out as a tree is but as the trunk of the tree only, which is what she did before sleeping—lay in the dark imagining her whole body as the trunk of a tree as she fell to sleep—well, she hadn't gone so far as to say that it would have made her uncomfortable, the size of the bed that was probably in the suite, she had merely been saying that it wasn't perhaps all that economic for someone such as herself when suddenly, on the windows on either side of the train, she had noticed all at once a whiteness, a thick, mottled white covering that you couldn't see out of, a mottled white almost like a snakeskin, which might have been condensation, or fog, or even frost, or some chemical that was being released into the tunnel and which she was thinking to ask the conductor about, if she could find him, find him to indicate to him that maybe it should be a concern—the whiteness on the windows—when again she noticed that the little roundish Swiss man was still on the train, and then she noticed that the window on her side was a clear black again, and then suddenly they were out of the tunnel and into an open valley—even though that valley was high up in the mountains—and the first thing she saw in the valley were little stone houses grouped together that were just nifty-looking, their smooth whiteish plaster walls and their little measured designs decorating them down the sides—and just as neat and practical as she had imagined Switzerland—and then, looking up, she saw the mountains, the mountains that she had come all this way for, the mountains rising and falling like huge white waves above her head, like white walls of water that were about to come foaming down on top of her, the mountains that were too high up for trees, too high up for those patches of trees to hold them in place, to hold those waves of snow, even though down here, where still she could see trees in patches, still they only looked like quills.

Well, hotels really were just hotels, she said to herself, following the bellboy to the suite.

Or to the room, rather.

And it was a good thing she knew all about those little things that are so important in traveling, like having every-thing ready just the way she had had it—the tips of her fingers, for instance, on the two francs that she'd just moved to her pocket, not wanting to have to be snapping her new purse open and snapping her new purse shut, not to mention scrab-bling all around in it looking for the right amount while the bellboy would be standing there on the door saddle not know-ing what to do and shuffling his feet.

Yes, even though some might find it a bit finicky, she was thinking—and opening up the suitcase that the bellboy had deposited so neatly on the little suitcase stand—a bit finicky to be traveling with one's own soap, or sleeping neatly over to one side of the bed even if that bed were a big one, a big one that some other kind of person would have come in and spread out all over, and always—even though one traveled alone—traveling with a robe; yes, given what had happened with the suite, and with the bathroom too, it hadn't served her too badly—had it?—her finickiness, or her prickliness, or whatever you wanted to call it.

Because if anyone was going to be inconvenienced by the situation, it would be least of all she.

Especially seeing as her toiletries were one thing about which she was always particularly organized, setting them up before she did anything else being one thing she was always making sure of. So that long before that other person would be ready, she'd be finished—that poor other person, the roundish man on the train, of all people, that typically Swiss-looking man, that poor man who'd been trapped in his gray suit all the way, looking all the way as if at any moment he'd be getting off their train, but instead had gone on along, no more able to get off than one could get off from those escalators in the flughafen, that poor man who'd probably been looking forward to a room and to a bath—to a bathroom, that is, that he didn't have to be worrying about sharing—looking forward to it a whole lot more than she.

And it was also a sign of her unruffledness—if that was even a word—that she had thought quickly enough to give that man at the desk, that helpful man whom she had confirmed as being the manager, a little something extra. Seeing that in her opinion the manager's apologizing about the suite, that his bringing up something unnecessarily disappointing such as that—disappointing to Mr. Garfield, that is—didn't need to be done. Seeing as she wouldn't be doing it either.

Because the first thing she had to do after she had finished getting her toiletries arranged on the table, the little marble table that was conveniently in that corner of the room near the bathroom door and not being used for anything, particularly convenient since she didn't want to be going in and out of the bathroom like a goose with its head cut off; yes, the first thing she had to do after she'd gotten her little things arranged neatly was sit right down and personally drop a note to Mr. Garfield, getting down to which was taking longer than usual, getting down to doing this note, being that this kind of note was sort of a new custom, so to speak—having to thank a parent directly, thanking him along the lines she'd been going over in the train, thanking him for everything, which had been *much, much too much, especially the suite,* she was thinking about beginning, although the subject of price, or of expense, rather—the *much, much too much*—wasn't right, now that she thought about it—although she had to allude to it just the same, the matter of *expense,* or *effort* was perhaps a better word, or *generosity in providing her with,* perhaps, although that wasn't quite right either, nor was *generosity in arranging for* quite right either.

She was sitting in the dining room of the hotel, in the nice, peaceful dining room of the hotel, and enjoying this little bottle of this delicious wine they had over here that was just like drinking a little soda water it went down so easily, this delicious light Swiss wine with the tiny little bubbles in it, this wine about which she was just thinking that even though she didn't usually take a chance with having any wine, here was a wine that *couldn't daunt a fawn.* Which was an even better little catchy way of remembering it, she was thinking, of remembering the pronunciation, now that she'd heard the waiter saying it aloud—*fawn daunt.*

Although she was going to wait another little bit to see if when the waiter said it again, there actually was that little tick of a *t* at the end that now she thought she hadn't heard.

Then she'd also had a little calf's liver, which she'd liked, especially when it was cooked the right way—not even the slightest little bit of purplishness if you cut into it.

And if you asked her, that little bit of seasoning, that little bit of schnapps, or whatever the maitre d'hotel had called it that you put in crêpes, hadn't put her even a feather's worth over the edge—not that she would have minded if it had, minded feeling a little airy, a little featherheaded, so to speak.

Because if it had done anything, it had made her not so bothered by the little prickly things that had been bothering her before dinner, the little nothing-things like the pillows, the pillows on the bed. Because even if there had been a little puff of dust that had come out of them when she'd plumped them, or which she had thought had come out of them, they weren't worth worrying over, anyway, the pillows.

But the main thing she wasn't worrying over anymore was whether she had gotten herself all ruffled up over that incident in the shower, by which she meant when the man had come in, the little roundish man whom she shouldn't have been surprised by at all, having been looking at him all day long on the train, and even on the plane, and having known, too, that he was in there—because of the confusion at the desk—in there, in the other half of the suite.

Because she hadn't.

Hadn't gotten all ruffled up.

But what had surprised her, though, was how sure she'd been—sure from the sound of the water of the shower having stopped, and sure from the sound of the door on his side closing—that he wasn't in there anymore and that he'd finished needing to come back in. Finished with the bathroom for good, or she would never have bothered to go on in there to get it—she blinked, blinked at the thought of it—to get the silly soap.

Well, it had been done quite smoothly, she was sure, the way she hadn't given up on it—the soap—or gotten all flustered trying to grasp it, trying to grasp it in the water that was left from his shower, but had said, "Oh, excuse me, I'll be out in a jiffy," and had just kept to it systematically, even after he'd left, kept to it as if it were nothing more than a geometry problem she was showing you how to keep to, following the little bar of soap here and there around the base of the shower as it glided its way ahead of her—not as if she'd pinched for it but with just the smooth little jumps of a watch with a quartz movement—and then having gotten it, how she'd picked herself up—although that wasn't quite it, the way to phrase it—and gone over to the door on his side and rapped on it and said in a chipper little voice, "All yours now."

And another thing she was rather proud about, now that she'd gone over it again in her mind, the incident in the shower, and seen that there was nothing in it that hadn't been done right—yes, another thing she was rather proud of was that line, the line that went *resting back against these pillows is like resting back against*—well, she didn't want to say *goose, goose* not sounding quite graceful enough.

And *swan* not being true.

Well, if you wanted to know the truth, it had happened so unexpectedly—what happened in the shower.

Because before she realized that he was standing above her in just his bathrobe—his bathrobe which, if you asked her, well, if you did ask her, it wasn't quite right for a bathrobe—because before she realized it, that he was standing above her, she had been down on her hands and knees in the shower not expecting the least little intrusion at all but just in the shower getting the soap and thinking about Switzerland, which is what the problem in the shower came down to, if there even was a problem—her thinking about all the ways of describing Switzerland, and her thinking about her line about Switzerland and the pillows. So that, instead of half-expecting something like this, what she'd done—even though *twitched-up* might not even be a word—was *twitched-up*. As if, from the back of her neck, a hair had been pulled.

She sipped a little wine.

Because that's, after all—the twitching—what had made the man move rather unexpectedly, which, if it had done it at all, had made the bathrobe rearrange itself just a little bit— which could have happened, although she wasn't sure it had, his bathrobe being a little too short, and of not quite the right material, being not quite heavy enough to stay hanging the way a piece of clothing ought to stay hanging, with the least little motion.

She sipped a little more wine. A little more of that delicious wine.

Of course, what you would see if you could see her here,

here in this dining room, was her sitting here with these little tables placed here and there equidistantly around the room, little tables at which little figures were all eating so nicely, and talking to each other all in such level tones, without anyone speaking so loudly that you could hear that person—including her little roundish man who had been surprised in the shower when he found her down at his feet and looking up—yes, gesturing and talking, raising their forks up to their mouths and back down to their plates and occasionally raising up their napkins, but doing nothing else, as if they were merely figurines in a small Swiss mechanical toy of some sort that could only keep on doing what they were doing.

Well, she probably shouldn't, but she had another sip.

And watched the tiny bubbles prickling to the surface.

In fact, shouldn't she be congratulating herself? Congratulating herself on the way that the day was not just behind her, behind her in the sense that it was past her in clock time, the way a clock passes something by, but that it was beneath her too, beneath her the way Switzerland had appeared to her just this morning from the airplane, with all of it way down below and very small.

Although not *it,* actually, but *they*—*they* being the parts of the day that just this afternoon had seemed so large.

They being the parts of the day that she had focused on so closely, parts like the pillows on the bed, the pillows which just before dinner had seemed to take up the whole frame of her vision, as if her vision were a rectangle—she liked this idea, she was testing it out, looking at what was before her in the dining room and seeing it in the shape of a rectangle, a framed rectangular picture in which those pillows she was talking about weren't any bigger now than that little train compartment of theirs had been—if you looked at it against the whole postcard of the mountains it had been coming up into.

Although that was not to say by any means that she'd changed her mind about the pillows.

Because a plain foam rubber pillow was still a lot more comfortable, in her opinion, and a lot more cleanly.

It was just that now, in this dining room, this dining room with its lovely high ceilings and its proportions so ample that no one was right on top of you; it was just that now those pillows, well, she didn't know how to describe it, how she felt different now about those pillows, those famous goosedown pillows which had surprised her with their heaviness, with their being so heavy that it seemed there weren't feathers in them but some other part of the goose's body, and their being twiggy too, twiggy because of the stems of the feathers that you could feel through the skin of the pillow cover, twiggy in a way that didn't let you think of light little clusters of feathers but more of the goose again, of the goose's body, than you'd want to think.

Which seemed ridiculous now, she had to admit, the picture of herself being pushed down onto those pillows as if she were just a puppet in a puppet show, and larger than life even; and it also seemed ridiculous, the thought of those pillows taking up the whole frame of her vision and not letting anything else of the room in, except a little on the sides, when in just a jiffy she could pick up one of those pillows and toss it lightly to the floor, or toss it into a letter, the letter to Mr. G., for instance: *those pillows, resting back on those pillows, resting on the back of those pillows.*

And you know, now that she thought of it again, it wasn't the surprise of the man coming into the bathroom or even the surprise of what she might have seen had the bathrobe opened just a little—which, if it had, she'd seen it before, what was in there, and countless times.

And not that she'd seen that much, either. Or that she'd even seen any.

Because when the bathrobe came open, it came open just a little, and in the shape of a V. Although not a V as in *V is for Victory.* But in an upside-down V. And not a wide one, either. Not a wide one as, say, the one birds go in on their way east, or south, or whichever way birds go to get away from the winter. And not that it came flying open, either—the edge of the bathrobe. Because if it happened at all, it was just in a little narrow sort of V, which he probably didn't even know was there.

No, it was just the surprise of how it looked, not in general but on this particular time—although the more she thought about it, she wondered exactly what she had seen—since it had been so little and for such a brief second that even the man himself, as she'd said, could hardly have known it; no, if it were anything, it was just the surprise that it looked not as it usually looked—*it* being the *thing,* that is. Well, not the *thing* but *things,* plural. Well, she'd say *pillows,* pillows being on the tip of her tongue anyway, even though that's not, of course, what they were; no, it was just the surprise, she was sure, of the way they looked, sort of darkish and with such pronounced little goose bumps, goose bumps which, now that she thought of it, were probably from his being cold, her poor little man in his natural bristles—by which she'd meant just his mustache when she'd said that; yes, it was just his being cold from that cold water, the remains of which had been still in the base of the shower when she'd been looking for her soap, that cold water and nothing else being the natural explanation for those little goose bumps and as well for the purplishness.

Which was giving her an idea, an idea for a little code with which she could put these things in her notebook. Because what she was bothering about now wasn't the incident itself—which had nothing in it to be ashamed of, she was sure, sure from having gone over it again in her mind, from having gone over it smoothly, the way the hand of a clock goes smoothly over all the little lines on its circle—what she was bothering about now being not the incident itself but how in her little notebook she was going to put it down.

Because every time she pictured being upstairs in her room and filling in that page of her little notebook—her little notebook with the clocks on the cover, those clocks which were so much like Switzerland—all she could picture was having the words fly off the page every time that page was opened to, they'd be so odd.

Except that now, now with these little jabs and darts starting up in her mind, these little jabs and darts of an idea for a little code to use in her notebook, a code to use so that with its strangeness her little incident wouldn't fly right up in your face like a bird, a bird that you were trying to catch the leg of; except that now she was getting the craziest idea, an idea that even this morning she would have blushed to have thought of, an idea for the craziest *Switzerland is* that anyone could have thought of, an idea which was rising up in her mind, each of its tiny little words, rising up almost like the bubbles in the fondant wine that she had just finished, rising up right to her fingertips and to her tongue almost, her nearly perfect little line—*with its purplish clouds, Switzerland this afternoon*—an idea which was rising up with such a little tingly feeling, all the jabs and darts of the description prickling up in her mind, that she'd like to get right up to the room to write them all down, to write them all down so that—as the little bubbles in the wine did when they got into the air—they wouldn't go away.

Well, she didn't know what she had been dreaming, it was rather confusing, really. But somehow, she thought, or she had just thought she had thought, that she had unzipped herself out of her dress, or that her dress, like a skin, had just unzipped itself from her, so that what she was in, she didn't know, nor did it matter, really, in the dream, because in the dream she was having, her gaze was like the gaze of a person who was going somewhere, of a person looking out.

But what she was conscious of, what she did know about, in the movie of her dream, was that the skin she had unzipped herself from had been folded, or she had folded it, into a sort of rectangle, and it was black and shiny, and beginning to inflate, and she was carrying it under her arm as one might carry a small painting, but one that was inflating.

Well, it was hard for her to keep remembering that this was a dream she was having, and that in the dream the inflated rectangle—and this part was very hard to understand, so she had to follow closely—and that in the dream the inflated rectangle had turned into a pillow, although it had a smell to it, and was prickly too, prickly against her cheek, as if there were little bumps all over it, a little like the bumps on the little rectangle, the little trapezoid of smoked eel, or maybe it was anchovy she was thinking of, anchovy with little bumps from where the little hairs were.

But the trouble was that she couldn't concentrate on the pillow because she was trying to reconstruct the very brilliant line she had just had about what Switzerland was, a line that began, *Switzerland is,* a line that began that way and had something to do with pillows, the pillow under her head, or the inflated rectangle—she didn't know—but the trouble was that while she had been trying to reconstruct her sentence about Switzerland, the thing that was rolling under her cheek felt as if there were something else rolling inside of it, so that it wasn't just the balloon which she had thought it was—with nothing in it but air, even though she had forgotten, it wasn't smooth either—but there was something in it she was trying to grasp, as she was trying to grasp her sentence, there was something rolling around under the skin of it that was very hard to grasp.

She sat up abruptly. She was sitting up and looking down at the white sheet underneath her.

At the plain white sheet underneath her.

The plain white sheet with nothing on it.

And what she had been dreaming, which now she could see was only a dream, was that she'd been sleeping not on this nice clean sheet, clean as the snap-on headrests on the train, but she had been dreaming that she was sleeping on a pillow that was purplishly dark, and had little bumps on it, and was squishy, having something inside it, like a gland, which had made her wake up, which had made her wake up straightening up so quickly that she thought her neck had been snapped, or that she had reentered life as another person, she sat up so quickly, so quickly from the horror of having to lie on such a pillow.

Which, as she'd been saying, was only a dream.

Which might have been exaggerated by the altitude.

Because she had heard that in a high altitude people had dreams.

And it also could have been, the rollingness and fullness of it, because she'd had a lot to drink. And that she hadn't, as she should have, been in to that bathroom.

Although, no, it was definitely not what she had first thought it was but simply something to do with the geese out on the little river, the geese that she'd been watching all that afternoon as she'd been doing her postcards, and also something to do with the pillows they had here in Switzerland—the twigginess of the pillows, and the unexpected heaviness of them, as if the feathers in the pillows had been plucked from the geese, leaving their bodies purple and squishy and marked by the little bumps where the feathers had been pulled.

Which had all been very naturally on her mind.

So she put on her robe, the nice matching robe to the nightgown that she had treated herself to especially for the trip, the robe and nightgown, which were a nice-feeling polyester blend, a practical one, and she listened at the door of the bathroom for no sound, and knocked on it softly, and listened again for no sound, and made her little trip into the bathroom and did what she had to do to sleep more comfortably.

And then, as quietly as she could, she unwrapped the little glass on the sink from its protective cellophane covering—because what she was, was extremely thirsty—and undid the plastic top of the bottled water, the Passuger water, or *wasser,* or whatever it said on the bottle, which, she had to admit, she had a little trouble not fumbling with—the plastic top of the bottle—which was maybe a little sign, she had to admit, of her having—although she thought she hadn't—drunk too much.

Then she made her way as quietly as she could back to the door, and tried to close the door as quietly as she could.

And then got back on the bed, this time leaving on her robe; and stretched up to turn off the light by the bed, and lay down on her stomach, her arms by her side, picturing herself as the dark trunk of a tree, darkening more as the light from the room went out of her eyes.

Which was what she had been thinking about when it began, a twitching and prickling all over her body as she lay there in the dark, a twitching and prickling that she first felt in her toe, then way up in her head, and down around the calf of her other leg after that, and then in an elbow, each of which—the twitches—made that part of her body seem to jerk, as if there were a spasm in it, which at first felt as if the bubbles in the fondant wine were coming to the surface here and there, having been reactivated somehow by the water she had drunk, and then she felt as if her body were the body of a puppet being jerked at its extremities, and then as if it were a clock, a clock jerking ahead second by second, except that it wasn't, the jerks not occurring in the circular order of a clock, or even the straight-line order of a clock stretched out straight, like the order of an escalator, which has, every second or so, those little jerks at the top for the person getting off; but the jerks, or the twitches, or the pricklings, were occurring with no particular order to them—one here, one there—as if all these jerkings, or twitchings, or pricklings, or whatever you wanted to call them, were mocking her, silly goose that she was, and that if she put her hand out to try to protect herself—now in one place, now in another—it would come somewhere else, the twitchings, the little bubbles coming up, or whatever it was.

Which she tried to stop by lying even straighter and with her arms at her side, her arms at her side as if they were part of the trunk of the tree, and trying also to keep her eyelids shut, because her eyelids, too, were twitching.

But no matter how straight she knew her body was, or how flat she knew she was lying on the firmness of the bed, or how tightly she had shut her eyes, she felt instead that she was drifting in space, in a black void, and spinning, and that her limbs were all unbranched and floaty as the stars—but no, not like the stars, no matter how hard she was imagining that, because when one of the stars prickled in the darkness, the other stars could still be seen spread out across all of the sky, whereas when the prickling came that was happening to her, it seemed that her body wasn't made of bones any more— bones that held the different parts of her at different distances from each other—but that all of her body had collapsed into nothing more than the very spot where the prickling was tak- ing place, or the jerking, or the plucking, which is also what it felt like.

And it wasn't regular in its timing, either.

Because she would lie still for a moment in the dark and nothing would happen.

And then suddenly it would happen again.

Although it was happening much less frequently now, the way a mechanism runs down, going forward a little, then stop- ping, then plucking forward again.

Which, even though the plucks were winding down, made them less pleasant than ever, seeming more violent and more disorienting in their unexpectedness. And even though she had no doubt that if she could wait longer, soon the pluckings would be over, or the twitchings, or the pricklings, slowing down as if they were taking longer, or someone were taking longer, or just plain *it* were taking longer—since *someone* didn't refer to anybody—taking longer and longer to locate where something was that was left to be plucked, still it was her opinion that more had happened today than she'd wanted to have happen; so that before she was all unplucked, so to speak, she'd turn back on the light.

And when she'd turned it on again and sat up again on the side of her bed, it was as punctual—well, she wanted to say, *as a star,* but since that was something she thought she'd heard before, she'd say, *as a train*—yes, it was that punctual, as punctual as her little Swiss train coming out into the open—that all the pluckings stopped.

For two hours now she had been sitting at her little desk by the window and looking out at the mountains above her coming into existence in their whiteness and their hugeness, the bed behind her made and all her belongings organized neatly in their places.

Because, in her opinion, there had been no point in turning off the light again and resting her head back down again if what it meant to rest your head was to sleep on those pillows, or to get that terrible jerking and plucking feeling happening again to her body.

Not that there had been anything wrong with her for having had it, for having had that dream.

Because it was a perfectly predictable dream that anyone could have had—no one else's pillow having any more feathers in it than hers had, so to speak; yes, it was a perfectly predictable dream that anyone could have had, considering the goose, and the wine, and not having gone in there to use the bathroom when she should have, not to mention the altitude—how much higher up she was than she'd ever been before.

Yes, it was just a dream—the dream of the little purple pillows—that anyone normal could have had, putting two and two together.

Well, it was past dawn by now, and speaking of pillows, the mountains in front of her had once again taken on their coverings from yesterday, which was to say that the nakedness of the night was now over, the day having put its feathers back on, so to speak, until it all seemed like Switzerland again: the mountains up there above her, every rumple and ridge and ripple of their white surface now articulated by the early morning sun, every rumple and ridge and ripple of them cascading over one another to form two huge wings of white water—not crashing down but just hanging there—and she, like some small and timid animal at its base not moving a muscle either, not even to write her postcards.

Except that in a moment, when the dawn was finished coming on, twitching—as it seemed to be doing—twitching ahead of itself at almost one hundred and twenty seconds at a time, she was going to get up, to get up because what she was going to do was unmake the bed she had just remade—which wasn't the most honest way of portraying herself, she knew that—because soon enough the person who would come in carrying the tray with her tea on it would be coming in, because in another moment it would be a decent enough time to be calling down for it, for the tea.

No, it wasn't the worst of things she could be doing, she was saying to herself, thinking of getting up in a moment and unmaking the bed not just on her side but also on the other side as well.

And so with the victory of the day come around again, with the lines of the small black trees that now she thought she could see on the surface of the mountains, the small black trees now standing as straight up as if they were the victory of the day applauding itself, and applauding itself also in the ripples and the ridges and the wildly tossing layers and layers of whiteness rising above her; and so with the victory of the day now come around again—with the mountains all covered in whiteness—she opened her little notebook with the clocks on the cover and began copying her nearly perfect little line down onto the postcard—*I do not think that I will ever sleep so well again,* she was copying from her little notebook, the movement of her hand across the postcard being nothing more than the twitching of some little kind of animal's eyes from edge to edge and back again, nothing more disturbing, against the monumental stillness of the mountains, than that little twitching—*I do not think that I will ever sleep so well again,* she was copying onto the postcard, *after the pillows here in Switzerland.* **Q**

Artichokes

The bus comes to a stop at Miles Point and the driver goes for Shumaker, waiting in his wheelchair in the fog, Shumaker doing his side-to-side dance and rolling his eyes all around—the thing the Shumaker does when someone is going to lift him from his chair in place and carry him somewhere. Shumaker's sister holds the chair while the driver lifts Shumaker's little body, and lets his stringy limbs hang down except for the hand that's always stiff in front, up under Shumaker's chin and turned away. The driver carries Shumaker onto the bus and he sits Shumaker in the seat across from Shumaker's sister. Then the driver starts driving again and he turns up the radio.

Shumaker rests his head on top of the stiff hand, and he looks out the window. Shumaker's head is too large for the rest of his body and, if it weren't for his being crippled, Shumaker would be handsome, except for the smirk.

They drive past artichokes that Half Moon Bay boys say look like cunts. When someone gets laid, Half Moon Bay boys say, "Get some choke?" They call each other cuntface. In the classroom when the teacher is there, they call each other chokeface.

Shumaker looks out of the window at the artichokes while the driver drives the bus.

Someday Shumaker's going to drive the fucking bus. He's going to drive the fucking bus up and down the highway spinning fucking wheelies that'll make the girls wet their pants. One day God's going to come onto the bus and tap Shumaker on the shoulder and say, "Gig's up, bud, you're normal now. I gave you the gimpiest body around because I knew you could handle it like nobody else could."

God's been talking to Shumaker late at night when every-body else is masturbating. Late at night, God comes into Shu-maker's room and bullshits about things. They sit and shoot the shit about women and about how someday Shumaker's going to be the best lay around, about how Shumaker's going to jazz a different girl every night, and how the girls are going to beg for more, girls that would not drop a stitch for anyone else.

Yeah, God's been talking to Shumaker late at night, about how one of these days Shumaker's going to fucking up and fly away and be it all.

"Heard you got a girlfriend," Shumaker's sister says to the driver from behind.

The driver keeps driving and Shumaker's sister asks for a piece of gum.

The driver reaches into his pocket and throws Mary Shu-maker a piece of gum.

"You bringing her to the dance Friday?" Mary Shumaker says.

Shumaker turns as far as he can turn and says it's none of her fucking business.

Mary Shumaker takes mascara out of her purse and rolls up her skirt until it comes above her knees.

The driver turns the bus into Moss Beach, and Mary Shu-maker has to lean across the aisle to hold Shumaker in his seat.

Shumaker does his side-to-side dance and rolls his eyes, looking pissed off and scared.

One of these days Shumaker's going to fly out of his fucking chair and do a dance right in the middle of the gym, and it will be like everything else was a dream and the thing that is happening is the only real thing. It'll be in the middle of Social Studies and all of a sudden God's going to come in the room and tap Shumaker on the fucking shoulder and say the gig's up and Shumaker can go be right. And Shumaker's going to just sit there for a few minutes just to show he doesn't care. Then he's going to stand the hell up and go hot-wire the coach's Jag so he can drive it to L.A. Shumaker's going to drive to L.A. and pick up a few fucking bitches on the way, dick them while he's driving, and maybe watch them while they're getting it off with each other in the backseat. Then Shumaker's going to hit the city and do a different bitch every night, and just play music—the music Shumaker has inside his head that's getting ready to blow it off and spray everybody dead.

Portuguese girls get up on the bus with their hair ratted high on top and with their eyebrows drawn on black, and Mary Shumaker holds her engagement ring up so everyone can see.

"Lenny Marsh?" the driver asks from his rearview mirror.

"Who else?"

"She's going to get knocked up so she can stay home and watch soap operas," Shumaker says. "Be one of those fat spics you see in the bank."

Mary Shumaker looks at her ring. The driver pulls back onto the highway. They can all smell the shit they put on the field for the artichokes.

"So when are you going to bring your lady out?" Mary Shumaker says to the driver. "Hear she's got a nice ass."

"Shut your cuntface," Shumaker says.

"This is your last year, isn't it?" the driver says to Shumaker.

"Yeah," Shumaker says.

"Then what?" the driver says.

"Get out of this fucking hole," Shumaker says.

"That's what everybody says," the driver says.

The fog gets thicker and the driver turns on his lights.

"That's what I said," the driver says.

"He got a scholarship to college," Mary Shumaker says.

"Why don't you shut your fucking face?" Shumaker says.

"No shit?" the driver says.

"Swear to God," Mary Shumaker says.

"What is he going to do with a scholarship?" the driver says.

Shumaker looks out the window at the artichokes. He looks at the artichokes and thinks about how the scholarship is only part of it, and about how they don't know the rest of it yet, the rest about God talking to Shumaker and about how this whole thing has been just one big fucking joke.

The driver pulls the bus up the hill to the high school, past the parking lot where students are smoking and making out in their cars. He opens the door and goes for Shumaker, lifting Shumaker up from his seat, and carrying him down the stairs to where Mary Shumaker has the wheelchair waiting.

Shumaker shifts from side to side and rolls his eyes all around and tries to move his arms and legs where they belong.

He looks at the driver. Shumaker says, "I am going to wipe my ass with it, asshole." Shumaker says, "You watch me wipe my fucking ass with it, asshole." **Q**

A Fragment from Two Case Histories

[1]

Freud's great English disciple, Dr. Forsyte, once remarked in a footnote in his edifying work *Psychoanalysis and the
Evolution of Upper Middle Class Taste* (Hogarth Press, 1937) that
a careful, meticulous venture through a gentlewoman's hand-
bag would yield to the adventurer as much insight into the
woman's character as would several years of analysis. Dr. Forsyte's disciple, Dr. Perry-Farrell, in turn remarked in a footnote to his article "The Meaning of Hairstyle" (19 *International
Journal of Psychoanalysis*, p. 237) that similar insight could be
gained from observing the contents of a woman's sitting room,
and with considerably less affront to conventional notions of
decorum and morality. This last suggestion occurred to me as
I climbed the stairs to the Récamier apartments.

Having been left by her butler at the door of her study and
advised to make myself comfortable, I instantly inferred that
Madame Récamier was obviously a woman for whom chairs
were very important. In the corner of the chamber farthest
from the door, I glimpsed in nearly perfect condition a chair
in the style favored by the revolutionaries of 1848, a simple,
unupholstered wooden chair with four legs, a flat seat, and a
high, three-rung back. Adjacent to this specimen and against
the wall farthest from where I stood was a high stool of the
variety preferred by cabaret singers as they sit, with micro-
phone, next to a grand piano. Continuing to look along the far
wall, my eyes took in a succession of chairs of the styles
popularized by a succession of late French monarchs, Louis
XIII, XIV, XV, and XVI, all ornately carved, generously padded, and with embroidered patterns upon silken seat and back
cushions. Lining the side walls were somewhat less impressive,
if no less functional, types—modern metallic folding chairs, a

few with white numbers painted across their slightly curved backs; worn-out wicker chairs whose seats seemed as if they had too often borne the weight of stout companions and now seemed as if they would scarcely succeed in accommodating small children; molded, one-piece plastic chairs with spindly metal legs such as one might find in hastily decorated offices. On one of the overcrowded bookshelves I detected a none-too-slender volume entitled *Chairs of the Orient;* on another, a monograph with the title *Seats of the Czars.* Curiously, in this amply dimensioned sitting room there was not a single sofa, nor even a loveseat; not a single item of furniture capable of holding more than one person.

As I considered what I observed and tried to determine what these clues might reveal to me of Madame Récamier's essence—whether a single great unifying principle of personality connected these disparate evidences that had been presented to my senses—my musings were interrupted by the appearance of Madame Récamier herself.

"Won't you sit down," she said, in a tone at once expressing both hospitality and stern authority. I chose a blue plastic chair on the side wall closest to the door. The spindly legs apparently were not all of equal length; consequently, the chair did not sit securely on the parquet territory beneath it. Rather than betray the slight, off-balance discomfort to which I had subjected myself by my unfortunate choice, I resolved to remain where I was. Madame Récamier remained standing, perhaps for a second or two longer than propriety permitted, before seating herself on the metal folding chair beside me.

"This has become my favorite chair, ever since my Queen Anne fell to pieces," she confided, disclosing more, perhaps, than courtesy required of a first interview.

"It does indeed have a most agreeable structure," I agreed, recovering quickly from my surprise at her decision to place us in such proximity. I saw that on her lap was an open pocketbook, and within it a hairbrush, a lipstick, and a multiplicity of other items of interest upon which, but for my good breeding, I would have lingered long enough to form a mental catalogue. Instead my eyes sought the bookshelves on the wall across from me.

"But I know you did not come here to discuss chairs," Madame Récamier said, "although perhaps another time you will." In her lifted eyebrows I read at once a hopefulness and a hopelessness.

"On the contrary," I replied, concealing my investigatory intentions under a mask of politeness, "there is nothing I would rather converse about."

"Very well," Madame Récamier said, as a servant deposited a tea tray before us. "A chair is a chair. Perhaps you agree?"

"Undeniably," I replied, but with a skepticism that, despite all of my efforts, might still have been manifest in the five syllables I had uttered. Her remark stirred up from its repose in my memory a statement Dr. Jones, in his three volume *Life of Freud,* attributed to the master himself, in which Freud admonished his followers that in rare but significant circumstances, namely, when between his own lips, cigars were simply cigars, and nothing more.

My fears of the transparency of my response were unwarranted, however. Madame Récamier continued as if we were in perfect accord as to her initial and major premise.

"A chair is a chair. Yet, you will not dispute, some chairs are more chairs than others."

"Absolutely," I said, this time with a total conviction that concealed my uncertainty of comprehension. If some chairs were more chairs than others, what were the criteria, I wondered, for making such a determination?

"Therefore," Madame Récamier concluded, "some chairs are less chairs than others. Your chair, for example, is less a chair than mine, since, evidently, you find it uncomfortable and a bit precarious. Not everyone finds it so, however."

Taking Madame Récamier's arguably impertinent public recognition of my lack of ease as an invitation to relocate, I rose, and having readjusted myself in the Louis chair on one side of Madame Récamier, I said, "It ought to follow, then, that some chairs are no chairs at all."

Madame Récamier made no attempt to suppress the laughter that filled the room with a high-pitched hilarity. "Do not be ridiculous," she replied, with a directness of expression I found unbecoming in a hostess, particularly in one addressing an unfamiliar guest. "Every chair is a chair."

I was impressed by the singularity of her logic. Her argument concerning chairs was both literal and practical, but possessed a certain subtlety not to be underestimated, it seemed to me, although, to be sure, her nicer distinctions presently eluded my full understanding. In the mere few moments of our interaction already I realized that Madame Récamier was a most mysterious and inscrutable subject.

"But I know you did not come here to discuss chairs," Madame Récamier repeated. "What are you here for?"

The true reason for my visit I could not reveal. I had come to Paris several months earlier to study with the great quasi-Freudian, Jacques LaTrache. Dr. LaTrache had invented and performed valuable pioneering research on the so-called long session. Unlike the customary therapeutic encounter, which had a duration of precisely fifty minutes, or the innovative "brief session," which was terminable at the pleasure of the analyst and very seldom exceeded five minutes, the long session, to quote from Dr. LaTrache's ground-breaking treatise, *Length and Width,* lasted "as long as it takes." In what I considered one of his most quotable comments, Dr. LaTrache had once—placing a hand upon my right shoulder and leaning over my left so I could feel his warm breath and wiry whiskers caressing my ear lobe—succinctly stated, "La quantity produces la quality." (Despite my assurances to the contrary, Dr. LaTrache was convinced that my knowledge of his native tongue was confined solely to an ability to recognize the masculine and feminine articles. Happily, Dr. LaTrache took great pleasure in speaking English, and he did so with considerable skill.)

Learning of my planned excursion to Paris, the orthodox Dr. Littleglove, my mentor at the British School, had attempted to discourage my interest in the French experiment, dubbing Dr. LaTrache's controversial technique as the "distended bladder method." From behind his vast, ashtray-covered desk, Littleglove had spoken with an uncharacteristic animation, abandoning his usual tone of reserve. "My good man, don't you see that what LaTrache is doing is nothing more than physiological blackmail? How you can possibly profit from attending on that crass vulgarian is beyond me. All he has to offer analysis is incivility." But having reached an impasse in the development of a therapeutic expertise, I resolved to make the journey, reasoning that nothing short of outright rudeness should be dismissed out of hand as improper analytic practice.

It could not be gainsaid, however, that the Frenchman's approach, even in his pomaded and manicured published account, presented much to offend those of delicate sensibilities, whether prospective patient or prospective practitioner. The tormented soul who might present himself to Dr. LaTrache for treatment was referred elsewhere if he would not assent in advance to depart each session only at the analyst's invitation. And during the pendency of each such session, the patient was denied leave to attend, however briefly, to his nonintrospective obligations, whether biological—hence Littleglove's pejorative appellation—familial, or vocational in nature, and regardless of the degree of urgency with which these obligations pressed their respective cases. "These restrictions," the LaTrache treatise explained, "have a twofold significance. First, knowledge that the analyst is willing to wait as long as necessary carries with it a sense of self-worth. The patient knows that what he has to convey is worth waiting for. Second, knowledge that one has certain societal responsibilities and corporeal needs that await the session's termination encourages full disclosure of psychopathologically germane material. For only such disclosure produces the desired permission to depart. Indeed, I have found that, with the exception of one or two incorrigibles, enough progress toward self-discovery is usually made within five minutes of their arrival such that my patients rarely need remove their overcoats." With a twinkling in his bespectacled eyes, Dr. LaTrache, taking me aside after a particularly brief therapeutic encounter, once remarked, "As soon as they realize that I have all the time in the world, they give up the fight and, as les Americans would say, 'spill their guts.'"

But the LaTrachian analyst himself was not similarly bound by the restrictions affecting his clientele. When faced with a stubbornly silent client, LaTrache did not hesitate to send for gastronomic sustenance, which he ate with particular relish before his salivating subject. His cluttered Champs-Élysées office, situated above a McDonald's restaurant, was littered with spent Egg McMuffin cartons. Nor did he hesitate, in full view of his patient, to disrobe and step into the shower stall adjacent to his rocking chair. Nor could the client even feel secure in his right to remain on the analytic couch; he was subject to being displaced temporarily by a subsequently scheduled patient or by Dr. LaTrache himself, if the latter felt a desire for sleep or amorous exercise. "The absence of restrictions on the analyst," the LaTrache treatise explained, "has a threefold significance. First, the patient realizes that although the analyst is willing to wait for worthwhile material to surface, nothing is gained by making him wait. The analyst sacrifices nothing. Second, by seeing the analyst go about the performance of his daily activities, the patient is reminded of what anxiously awaits him once he has relinquished his required quota of secrets. Third, the patient discovers in the analyst a model of openness and disclosure, for the analyst stands ready to reveal all, to live in the patient's fishbowl, as it were. It is a rare client on whom these lessons are lost."

If it is a rare patient who is able to resist the pressures of the LaTrache technique, it is a rare analyst who is capable of fully inflicting those pressures. Often, as I worked under his supervision, LaTrache leaning over my left shoulder, as was his wont, I gave in and allowed my patients a respite in the restroom or a few minutes to pacify their crying children in the antechamber. I am embarrassed to say that many times I ignored strong sensations of hunger rather than be observed in the act of ingestion, and once when LaTrache, always the great teacher, suddenly disappeared and reappeared with a very saucy strumpet, I waved her away rather than join with her in a carnal caress on the patient's couch. But Dr. LaTrache was quite tolerant of, even amused by, my squeamishness, my "surfeit of good manners," and what he sometimes called my "British ways." "Even Americans," he reassured me, "who can be so gauche"—here he was using the word as it has been received into English—"are slow to learn my methods." Indeed, as I soon discovered, Dr. LaTrache considered me a most promising pupil.

Called into his office one day, I perceived on LaTrache's countenance a look of fatigue and frustration. "Perhaps I have been too long among le French so I no longer understand them. I need what you call a second opinion about this Madame Récamier of mine. *Mon dieu,* she is one tough nut to crack." Dr. LaTrache continued to astonish me with not only his skill in speaking proper English, but also with his knowledge of the American idiom. "She comes into my office, she sits down, and all she talks about is furniture. My chairs, her chairs, the minimum set of attributes of the generic chair, Le Corbusier on chairs, the Platonic versus Aristotelian debate over the superiority of the chair versus the bench. I am interested in the heart, the seat of the emotions; and the brain, the seat of the repressions; but Madame Récamier, all she is interested in is seats. What am I going to do with such a patient as this? She exasperates me. She can outwait me. Finally I can stand it no longer and I send her home to her house full of furniture. And what have I learned about her that is, to use that ridiculous term that I lifted from God knows where, 'psychopathologically germane'? Zilch. What am I going to do with this Madame Récamier? I thought you might go pay her a visit, look her up, let me know what you make of her. Find some pretext. Tell her you have some interesting African eight-legged chairs, and you heard she was a noteworthy collector of such specimens. Tell her you have some antique slip covers made for Marie Antoinette. Tell her anything."

"I am here on a pretext, I must confess," I responded to Madame Récamier's abrupt inquiry. "Your butler erroneously believes me to be a seller of rare chairs. I knew of no other means of gaining an audience with such an esteemed collector as yourself. I hope you will forgive me this minor trespass into the territory of deceit. I am sure you will not regret having received me."

"You're English, aren't you?" Madame Récamier interrupted. "I don't believe I presently own an English chair. Do you have any? My late husband despised the English. 'English chairs,' he used to tell me, when I made my periodic applications for funds for interior decorating, 'are like English food. Inedible.' He had his reasons, of course, for despising the English. Who, I ask you, does not? Still, a good English chair in his house would not be such an affront to his memory as to be out of the question, would it? So do you have any?"

I realized that Madame Récamier, in her monomania, had quite completely ignored my attempted confession. "As a matter of fact, I do," I replied, quite surprising myself with my response. "You mentioned Queen Anne as a monarch whose furniture you hold in particular favor, did you not? I have recently been offered several specimens in virtually mint condition: a footstool, a divan—"

"I have no interest in those pieces," she quickly interrupted, cutting me off in midsentence in a manner to which I was most unaccustomed. "Do you have any chairs?"

"I'll inquire of my suppliers."

"You do that. And be quick about it. In matters of this kind, I have always found that time is of the essence."

"I'll do my utmost, you may be certain of that," were the words that somehow formed on my lips. "But while I'm here, I have at my disposal some fine Georgian accessories—some curtain rods and area rugs, as well as a well-designed and very sturdy sofa."

"A sofa? What do I want with a sofa?" my hostess exploded. "Do you have any idea how regularly I have to bear these vexatious visits? All manner of merchants manage to get past my butler on the pretext of having something I can use, and then, once in the door, all they offer me are those oversized, overstuffed sofas. Did you come here to discuss chairs or not?"

Before I had an opportunity to compose a reasonable response to this inquiry, I found myself dismissed. "I don't want to see your face around here until you have some information about chairs. Chairs! Is that clear?"

[11]

Freud, in the opening chapter of *Civilization and Its Discontents* (Hogarth Press, 1930), endeavored to illustrate the structure of the mind by comparing it to the architectural traces of ancient Rome. He observed that whereas in the Eternal City the more recent architecture is built upon, and conceals, the ruins of older edifices, in the mind spatial relations are more complex: the relics of the old mental processes, while providing the infrastructure for the new, continue obstinately, in addition, to occupy the same field as the new; and the ancient and the modern virtually vie for this common ground, now one and now the other thrusting itself before the startled gaze of the observer. Dr. Hyphen-Smith, the great Freudian archaeologist, in his 1942 "Shopping for Buried Treasure" (38 *Proceedings*), in turn observed that for those without the means to undertake a guided excursion through the back alleys and excavations of the Italian capital, a similar, albeit equally imperfect, insight into the mental topography could be afforded by a brief trip to almost any antique shop in England. This last suggestion pushed itself into my consciousness as I pushed past the heavy door of Pierre's Period Chairs.

For notwithstanding that I was far from those somewhat chaotic British establishments to which Dr. Hyphen-Smith adverted, I nevertheless found myself confronted with a quite passable metaphor for the human mind, or making some allowances for national differences, at the very least, for the French mind. The chairs in Pierre's were not arrayed in neat rows across the shop's ample floor space, or stacked in orderly vertical rows up to the shop's ceiling. Rather, the shop's stock of furniture, which, despite the establishment's name was not limited solely to the specimens with which Madame Récamier was so thoroughly absorbed, was displayed in a most unusual manner. Sofas, chairs, armoires, dressing tables were piled atop one another in a single interconnected mass—the legs of one piece pushing through the seat of another, a torn swatch of foam or fabric seeming to serve to cover two or three unrelated surfaces, a back-rest broken from its moorings and haphazardly traversing the rippling waters of space and style— a mass that greatly resembled an early Cubist exercise, which on my visits to the Tate sometimes left me feeling oddly at sea.

"What are you here for?" The proprietor's inquiry jolted me out of my reverie.

"A chair."

"Any particular kind of chair?"

"It makes no difference," I answered. "After all, a chair is a chair, *n'est pas*?" Out of character, I laughed out loud at my little private jest. My laughter, regrettably, was not infectious. But I was not unprepared for this humorlessness.

"Those antique dealers are a grim bunch," LaTrache had warned me. "Worse than priests. Don't ask me why." We had been discussing my interview with Madame Récamier. "So, I see that she threw you out on your ear. Ah well, don't take it personally. That's Madame Récamier for you. As I say in my book, or maybe it's in one of my articles—maybe I never said this before—you win some, you lose some. Now I remember, I read it in Sartre."

My curiosity having been aroused, I was less willing, however, to let the matter die so quick a death. "All is not yet lost," I protested.

"That famous British stiff upper lip. I see you partake of that peculiar national trait. Well, go ahead. I'm all ears."

"This restricted focus, this obsession, perhaps, with chairs. I cannot help but suspect that such a distinctive and pronounced pattern of response must be laden with meaning. What I would propose, with all due respect, is that rather than endeavor to work around the chairs, it would perhaps be profitable to work through them."

"Ah, to be relatively young again! To have such energy, such fervor, such insight. I was a young analyst myself once. Did you know that? Before I grew this pain in the neck of a beard that our illustrious founder mandated for all middle-aged practitioners. I remember back then I had a real fruitcake of a patient, a lot like Madame Récamier. At the time, all I had was a mustache. This man, according to his bewildered wife, had a thing about fire hydrants. Couldn't walk past one without bursting into tears, although sometimes instead of crying he would spit. Well, when I found this out, naturally I went right out and got a fire hydrant and put it in my office so when this guy came he could, as you say, work through his feelings. I had all kinds of theories. But I could never get him to talk. He was too busy clearing his throat all over my office. Anyway, finally one day I had a brainstorm and I sent the guy to an allergist, and that was that. Of course, sometimes it pays off to spend your time on these details as if they hold the key to the organism. You want to pursue this Madame Récamier business? Be my guest. But don't forget: just as those who make their beds must lie in them, and those who light lamps subject themselves to their harsh incandescence, so those who would deconstruct or reconstruct chairs may find themselves having to sit in them. My God, how perfectly put. I better go write that down. There's still time to make a place for that in my second edition. I wonder if there's anything else I can add to that. Those who build fires . . . Nah, too obvious."

Faint as it was, that was all the encouragement I required. That very afternoon, immediately following tea, having the benefit of several sundry sources—including Dr. LaTrache, Madame Haitek, my concierge, *Lloyd's International Registry of First-rate Secondhand Furniture Emporia,* and the *Parisian Purple Pages,* a sort of underground interior decorators' guide I had purchased cheaply at a riverbank bookstall—I compiled a comprehensive list of those shops where I might locate the item that would ease my readmittance to the Récamier rooms. And the next morning I began the actual search itself.

Even before my Parisian sojourn, secondhand furniture shops were already a class of shops with which I had more than a passing familiarity. Financial difficulties—the result of unanticipated legal complications in the distribution of my father's estate—had forced me to vacate my spacious Hyde Park apartments for a cramped, unfurnished room in a district of the city better left undesignated. Naturally, to save what little I had for my studies, I had acquired what little furniture I needed from London's junk dealers.

Secondhand furniture shops also occupied a prominent place in my unconscious life because they have consistently appeared from my late adolescence and nearly into the present in a frequently recurring dream. This dream I never reported to my training analyst, having, prior to analysis, satisfied myself that no significant aspect of my nocturnal fabrication had escaped my comprehension. The cloak of anonymity that these pages provide persuades me, however, to permit my dream to see the light of day.

. . .

It is quite late in the evening, approaching midnight. I am sitting alone at a bar, a bottle of ale before me. An attractive woman sits down beside me and we begin talking. She looks at her watch, notes that it is getting quite late, and suggests that I accompany her home, her suggestion taking a rather lewd form. Although startled, I nod my assent, and we depart. She takes my hand.

Walking along the streetlamp-lit streets, silent now, our path is crossed by a flight of beautiful exotic birds. Later, our path is crossed by a pack of bony, hungry dogs with tired, wet, baleful eyes.

Presently, we stop in front of a secondhand furniture store, piled from floor to ceiling with loose arms and legs, jutting at crazy angles from their respective bodies. My companion tells me she resides above the store, one flight up. As we climb the stairs, her hand closes on my arm and she kisses me with burning lips; and looking into her face I see that, far from being attractive, she is unspeakably ugly. I bolt down the stairs and out the door.

Variation 1: We enter my companion's apartment and are greeted by her parents. We sit down to dinner, during which my companion's beauty returns.

Variation 2: We enter my companion's apartment, she disrobes, and as she stands naked before me, it is apparent that my companion is a man.

Variation 3: We enter my companion's apartment, we disrobe, and couple like animals.

"Sir, what are you here for? I hope you did not come here to discuss philosophy. Does this place look like the Sorbonne?"

In truth, the shop did bear more than a slight resemblance to the Sorbonne, which, since the student demonstrations, had become as intellectually disheveled as Pierre's was materially disheveled. I did not, however, reveal this insight to one so concrete and unmetaphorical in his thought processes as I surmised this antique dealer to be.

"I am interested in purchasing a fine English chair, preferably a Queen Anne, preferably one not in such disrepair that it is beyond restoration, and one of high enough quality so as to satisfy the demands of a most demanding customer."

The proprietor squinted at me through his dusty spectacles. "Such a chair I sold not five minutes ago. All of a sudden a run on English furniture. Who would have thought that was possible? Chairs that force you to sit like a statue, sofas only suited for stiff family portraiture, even the carpets are hard on the feet. Such furniture is only good for firewood, except that English wood does not burn well. Of course."

I listened to this somewhat unflattering assessment of my nation's achievements in the decorative arts with my usual good grace. "Be that as it may, do you expect to have available for sale any other specimens of the type I have heretofore described?"

"Oh, yes. I am sure I have several, down near the bottom." He gestured toward his dense stock of wares. "Just give me a day or two. It's not so easy to remove a piece without upsetting the organic unity of the work. This isn't just a furniture shop, you see, but an artistic statement as well, and one I must dismantle and reassemble with the greatest of care."

If Dr. LaTrache had been among the French too long, I obviously had been among them too briefly. Apparently there were more differences between the French and the English than I had imagined. Certainly, the *petit bourgeois* English merchant did not view his merchandise in anything but economic terms. Indeed, as my mentor Dr. Littleglove frequently took pains to point out, the middle classes' fundamentally economic cast of mind made them dreadful candidates for analysis.

"But don't worry, I'll figure it out," the proprietor continued. "So why don't you come back tomorrow and see what I have for you. In the meantime, let's hope this English mania comes to a stop. I must admit, I've never much understood the

peculiar whims of the collectors I service, although, in retro-
spect, their tastes often seem like a sign of the times. In this
case, not a very promising sign. But maybe I am jumping the
gun. Could be just a fluke, of no statistical significance. Well,
we'll see. Now you better get out of here. I know you wouldn't
want to witness the agonies of destruction and creation that lie
ahead for me. I doubt you have the stomach for that, having
been reared, no doubt, on that unconscionably bland food.
Now get out and don't come back until I'm ready for you."

As I passed out into the bright light of midmorning, I
looked back for a second at the shopkeeper in his dreary space.
He stood before his pile of odds and ends and laughed.

[III]

Consistency of form dictates that I should begin this
chapter as I have begun the previous two, with a learned observation from a learned practitioner, followed by a learned cor-
ollary from a learned corollarist. Yet, at this juncture, perhaps
it would not be unseemly to depart from this pattern, if for no
other purpose than to demonstrate the virtues of flexibility.
To quote again from Dr. LaTrache's treatise—and this quota-
tion would appear to have application even outside the analytic discipline—"Rigidity breeds flaccidity."

It was a certain rigidity in my analytic technique—to which
I have alluded earlier—that caused me to seek out Dr. La-
Trache. And it was indeed a certain rigidity in my charactero-
logical composition, as evidenced by my wardrobe, that the
Parisian detected even during our first interview.

"Loosen up, man. Don't sit there so stiffly. And take off
that tie. Here, give it to me. And that tweed jacket with the
elbow patches. I'll take that too, and stick it in my closet. And
the vest, and the shoes. Hmm . . . we seem to be the same size.
Here, put on my sneakers." Not a quarter of an hour into our
meeting and Dr. LaTrache had me reduced to my undergarments.

I was soon to learn that, although he did not insist on it

as a necessary precondition to psychotherapy, Dr. LaTrache strongly encouraged his clients to leave their apparel, save their undergarments, in his waiting area. As the LaTrache treatise explained in an appendix entitled "Optional Reading, not Important"—an appendix to which I had inadvertently neglected giving my fullest attention prior to arriving in Paris—

"The shedding of outer clothing has a threefold significance. First, and so obvious that it barely bears mention, the stripping down to one's Jockeys is a concrete example of the stripping away of one's defenses and the getting to the heart of the matter. I have frequently found that once the patient has taken the step of stepping out of his trousers or jumping out of her jumper, he or she becomes much less reticent, and the analysis often takes a quantum leap forward.

"Second, one's undergarments quite often provide a truer picture of one's mental life than one's outergarments. The latter, after all, are usually worn to please others: bosses, spouses, circles of friends and associates. Everyone dresses for success, to use the latest sartorial jargon. Whereas underwear is personal. One answers to no one for it; the wearer gets to please himself, to live out his own little desires. I am no longer surprised by clients wearing bright red satin panties or boxer shorts sporting dollar signs or bloomers booming forth with printed assessments shared by the manufacturer and the purchaser: HOT-TEST STUFF IN TOWN or TRY IT, YOU'LL LIKE IT or NO ADMITTANCE. Not only does the therapist gain a great deal of information from what he observes of the client's underwear, but the client, realizing that the therapist is making significant observations, does not want to be misunderstood, so he soon augments the therapist's observations with explanations of his own.

"Third, unlike outerwear, which when soiled is immediately packed off to the cleaners, underwear is permitted by most wearers to retain its stains. Many of my clients—who, after all, are fairly representative of clients everywhere—do not dress for dinner. Rather, they undress, for greater comfort; and, inevitably, loose food particles and cooking juices land on their second skin. And even those of my clients who do dress for dinner don't bother to blot out the traces of appetite that soak through their third skin onto their second. It goes without saying that the analyst may learn much from studying his patient's eating habits, which he may easily do once his patient has stripped down. Often I have been able, for example, to spot the faded presence of alleged aphrodisiacs or detect an unacknowledged obsession with marinara sauce. Furthermore, the study of the stains produced by substances from the patient's own body may also yield valuable insights. Nor should the analyst fail to take note of underwear that is inexplicably spotless, or of a body that, stripped to its underwear, turns out to be wearing none."

Looking over my undergarments, Dr. LaTrache exclaimed, "My God, man! You're as uptight inside as you are outside." Indeed, his conclusion was not unjustified, given the spotless, starched appearance of my apparel. "Where is the mess about you?" he asked, presumably rhetorically. "Your poor patients! I bet you have one of those book-lined offices with one of those black, serious couches that feels like concrete to lie on, with a sandpaper napkin under the head; I bet your professors are trying to teach you to smoke cigarettes in a holder or one of those noxious pipes—you're too young yet for a cigar—so your people can't even breathe."

I meekly conceded the accuracy of his wager, meanwhile trying to form an impression of his office and the intelligence that had assembled such a motley collection of objects. Strewn across one low table were what seemed to be American baseball cards.

"May I?" I asked, indicating the table, and my soon-to-be mentor nodded. I stepped over and around piles of debris. My initial speculation was correct. Kurt Bevacqua, Cleveland Indians, infield-outfield. Ruben Amaro, New York Yankees, shortstop. Hector Lopez, Dick Schofield. What was special about these athletes? "Why do you keep these cards?" I inquired.

"Why not?"

"Who are these players?"

"Nobodies. Somebody's heroes maybe."

"I see."

Another table held a bowl full of dried lemons and limes, peach pits, and yellowed newspaper clippings. I picked up one of the clippings. GARAGE SALE, the headline proclaimed. AGRICULTURAL PRICES UP. ACCOUNTANT STILL ON THE LOOSE. MAN BITES DOG. DOG BITES MAN. TUESDAY: COME SEE SARAH THE MULE-FACED WOMAN.

"These appear to be randomly selected stories," I observed. "Indeed, some are not stories at all."

"That's right. And why should it be otherwise?" Dr. La Trache inquired. "I'll bet you've never seen such beautifully dried citrus. Oranges are trickier, I haven't gotten the hang of that yet. An old Lebanese taught me the secret of preserving the lemons and limes. Take a whiff."

I inhaled. "A most agreeable, delicate scent," I opined.

"Precisely," Dr. LaTrache exclaimed. "And there is an unconscious message in that, which, I hope, is not lost on my clients: that which is delicate may be agreeable." I could not discern from his tone or from the reflection off his spectacles whether he was joking or in earnest. "So often they come here to discuss quote-unquote delicate matters with a heavy heart, like it's the end of the world: something they've seen, something they've done or haven't done. But it's not the end of the world. 'We can talk about it,' I'm trying to tell them, 'and something good may come of it all,' like the sweet aroma coming off those old shriveled fruits. The past, properly preserved and resurrected, is more than just a source of pain."

"I see."

"I'm curious," said Dr. LaTrache, pulling at his beard. "Just how do you discuss quote-unquote delicate matters with your people?" I'm certain Dr. LaTrache noticed the dilation of my pupils and the beads of perspiration forming on my temple. "I've always believed that if they are worth talking about, delicate matters must be discussed indelicately— How should I put this to one like you?—by using, let's say, the language of the gutter. Otherwise we never know what we're talking about and the discussion is like a striptease." I recalled a chapter of *Length and Width* entitled "Calling a Spade a Spade."

Perhaps to save me embarrassment, although he had not spared me earlier—he may have intuited a line he deemed it inappropriate or unprofitable to overstep—Dr. LaTrache himself answered the question he had put to me. "I bet you encourage your clients, whatever their natural inclinations, to speak in the style of those Henry James novels where you never know what's what. 'Problems with my husband,' your client confesses. And you know what kind of problems she's talking about. And she's just waiting for you to let her tell you all about it: how his putz is too small, how he makes her swallow it, et cetera. But instead, you look at her like she's out of line to burden you with such things, you stare at her, light a pipe, and finally, three sessions later you make a vague reference to her 'intimate relations.' By then, she knows better than to bring it up again. Maybe she'll say something vague about 'lovemaking not being pleasurable' and that's the end of that, as far as she's concerned. But now you're starting to become titillated by her story and begin asking her questions that sound like a class in Greek mythology. 'Is it that you feel like Persephone when you would rather be Diana?' 'Impossible as it sounds, do you think maybe your husband is looking to you

to be his Ganymede, or looking elsewhere for his Ganymede?'
Now what is your poor client supposed to make of all this,
other than to think you've lost your marbles or that you're
getting your kicks at her expense? Don't forget, it's fucking
we're talking about here, not mythology."

All I could do was admit that the doctor had rather too
faithfully described my clinical practices.

"But," said Dr. LaTrache as he concluded our interview,
"don't worry. Your problem is that you never saw your mother
naked. But even that can be overcome. There's a lot for you
to learn. But, after all, what are you here for if not to learn?"

[IV]

Thoughts of death often overtake me. In my dreams
and my waking hours. Death by fire. Firearm. Drowning. Violence, torture. Disease: leukemia brain tumor kidney failure.
Quick slow. Funerals, Attended unattended.

I am walking along a street lined with skyscrapers. A telephone directory that has fallen from a window ledge descends
at an angle and speed permitting it to pass right through me,
back to front, clearing every organ in its path. I am hurled in
front of a speeding subway car. I quietly pass during the night.
Autopsy inconclusive but no foul play suspected. Foul play
hinted at in expurgated excerpt of coroner's report.

I am gunned down, gangland style, as I walk out my front
door onto the street. Car speeds off machine guns spraying
spare bullets at streetlamps and garbage cans. There is talk,
disbelief, speculation. A case of mistaken identity? Not so un-
common: the syndicate is less careful about that these days. Or
did he have a secret life, a side unknown, unglimpsed by even
his colleagues. Drugs gambling loan-sharking unpaid bills. Ac-
counts settled. Scores settled, tit for tat. No one can be sure.

What, when all is said and done, are obsessive thoughts of
death? There is a fairly extensive body of literature on the
subject. For a good introduction to the classical position, the
reader may wish to consult Helene Deutsch's case history "A

Life Unlived" in *Adventures in Analysis,* ed. by A. A. Brill (Harcourt Brace Jovanovich, 1962).

[v]

As for the second time I climbed the stairs leading to the Récamier apartments—this time laboring breathlessly under the weight and bulk of my prize from Pierre's, a rather perfect Elizabethan armchair the likes of which scarcely could be seen even in Buckingham Palace—as I struggled to retain my balance and keep my gasps from becoming too audible, I was reminded of a digression Geza Roheim once allowed himself in his ground-breaking *Psychology of Music.* "The burden on the child's mental life in seeing his mother naked," Roheim wrote, "is not unlike that borne by a man of only average strength who attempts to carry a piano up seven flights of stairs." Strangely enough, Dr. Brutus French Smith, the eminent piano mover, picked up on, and turned rather on its head, this (for Geza Roheim) insignificant comment. In his ground-breaking instruction manual, *Lift and Separate,* Smith made the following observation: "As a man of only average strength, I must admit that the feeling of accomplishment I get upon successfully carrying a piano up seven flights of stairs is great indeed. By the time I reach the top landing, I feel almost as I remember feeling when, four years old, I saw my mother naked. Indeed, sometimes as I approach that top landing, I can almost see my mother naked." It required no less a thinker than Dr. Littleglove himself to reconcile these two statements. My teacher had, in his younger days, been considered, among other things, the foremost analyst of piano movers. Eventually he had had to abandon this highly specialized practice. "The strain was enormous," he once confided to me privately. In a footnote to a footnote entitled "Order Out of Disorder: Answering My Critics," Littleglove tersely stated, "While seeing his mother naked may, retrospectively, seem quite an accomplishment to a piano mover, it is the sort of accomplishment whose burden weighs so heavily as to suit its victims for only the most brutish forms of manual labor." End of footnote, case closed.

Clearly, Dr. LaTrache did not completely share the assessment of Roheim and my teacher. I wondered which view was correct as I staggered under my load.

Dr. LaTrache, at our first meeting, had, of course, accurately guessed that I had never seen my mother unclothed. But prior to that time, I had never suspected that this was a bad thing, a lamentable circumstance. My intuition and the weight of respected analytic authority had indicated otherwise. As had my father.*

Indeed, I was to learn many years later that my father's injunction did not apply to me alone. On his deathbed, my father lifted himself up on his elbows and leaned over to me and said, "One thing, perhaps the only thing, I'll go to my grave regretting, my boy, other than not having spent enough time with my business—I never saw your mother in an advanced state of undress. Oh, what the hell. That I never saw your mother naked. Buck-naked."

But now, as I staggered under the weight and bulk of my armchair, I looked to the top of the final flight of stairs and realized that my progress was being scrutinized by Madame Récamier, standing on the landing, naked; and looking, despite the obvious differences in age and nationality, strikingly similar to my mother as I remembered her looking in my youth, the face showing the same arched eyebrows and full lower lip, the same long graceful neck and full breasts, the same small hips, and presumably, extrapolating from above to below, the same reddish-blonde pubic hair.

"Won't you sit down," she said, once I had completed my

---

*When I had just attained my third birthday I was told that my father was waiting to speak with me in his study and that I must go in without delay. He had me pull a chair close to his own, and when I had settled myself he leaned down and looked hard into my eyes and said, "You must never enter your mother's room while she is dressing." Terror-stricken, I asked how I would know when she was dressing. "Never enter your mother's room unless called. Discretion is the better part of valor, my boy. You may go now."

climb and all but flung the chair onto the carpet of her sitting room. Her tone carried the same mixture of friendliness and harsh assertiveness that I had noted on my first visit and left me unsure of how to react; I reverted to ancient habits.

"I'm not sure I should stay," I stammered. "Don't you believe it is highly improper to receive mere acquaintances in such an advanced state of undress?"

"Oh, rubbish," Madame Récamier replied, doing her best to imitate the sound such words would produce coming from the mouth of a native Englishman. Her lips opened into a smile most accurately described as playful. "Who says it's improper? It's my house." A cup of tea was handed to me. "So you have not returned empty-handed. Very well. Let's have a look."

As Madame Récamier leaned over my chair, I could only intermittently avoid directing my gaze, it embarrasses me to say, at her. "The legs are very well preserved, I see," she commented. "And the arms are most exquisitely shaped." The same, I reflected, could be said of Madame Récamier, who, although widowed, seemed quite youthful.

She circled the chair a couple of times, her excitement quite evident in her wordless exclamations. "But," she abruptly terminated her inspection, and true to the criteria she had enunciated on my previous visit she asked, "How is it to sit on? Have you tested it?" I had to admit that I had not. "Well, what are you waiting for?" Grasping me by the shoulders, Madame Récamier gently but forcefully pushed me backward into the valuable antique. Made more than a little self-conscious by her stare, I adjusted and readjusted myself on the cushions, crossing my right leg over my left and my left leg over my right, leaning forward and backward, trying out each arm, sitting on the edge of the seat and within its depths. "Well?"

I chose my words, on such a critical subject for my hostess, carefully. "A chair if ever there was one. Very much a chair."

"Let me try it," Madame Recamier demanded, her excitement mounting, a slight but readily perceptible flush pervading her throat and torso, and I hastily rose to accommodate her. "Oh my! Who would have thought . . . ? It's perfect. The answer to my prayers. Finally . . . Thank you so much. Tomorrow I can call a moving man to clear out all this junk, and maybe I can start to look at sofas again. . . . Young man?"

I turned. I had been standing, with my back to Madame Récamier, leafing through the pages of a book I had hastily taken down from a shelf and whose words made not the slightest impression on my consciousness, and looking out from the window onto a sunny courtyard full of benches, one occupied by a pair of avid adolescents.

"And how do I look in it?"

Some part of me I had seldom encountered spontaneously responded. "Lovely. Like someone in love. Like someone to be taken to bed—shall we?"

Madame Récamier stood and took my hand. "I don't see why not. And considering all you've done for me, that's the least I can do, I suppose. Besides, how long must I wait? It's been long enough, too long. After all, what are women here for?"

[VI]

One final footnote.

"I don't know how you did it, but Madame Récamier is cured," Dr. LaTrache announced a couple of days after my second visit. "She came in for her session, and she was in and out. Less than thirty seconds. Didn't even sit down. But it was long enough. I could see right away that there's nothing troubling her, so I signed her release papers. (Regarding the use of commitment and release documents in the LaTrache method, see *Length and Width*, pp. 19–21 and Dr. Littleglove's critique, "Slavery and Manumission," in 78 *Proceedings*.)

"And by the way," Dr. LaTrache added, "you seem somewhat better yourself." **Q**

The Burnt

It was at the end of the summer of sunburnt-yellow lawns, of cracked-plastic green garden hoses and saltwatered showers at the beachside path that the Inland Winds came one night, carrying the fires one house closer to our house, to the neighbor's house that we, the whole entire neighborhood of people I had never before seen so gathered at once, stood in the graveled street, barefooted in bedclothes blowing up and loose in the heated wind the tops of the long-leafed drooping trees blew swayedly in, as the neighbor's house burned roof to ground, backward from the ground-to-roof way I had watched the house get built taller and wider than any other house in all of our town, to what was now an empty, blackened brush of land where the laddered high-dive, blue swirl slide of the swimming pool still stands.

After that night came the off-work last holiday of summer, with my parents and the next-fence-over parents oiled bodily in swimsuits, air-blown ashes stuck to their skin as the parents lounged on the lawn on barbecue-sauced blankets held down against the winds by the jugs of drink the parents were pouring tall ones they drank on from, talking, "That's what happens when you build such monstrosity of house, blocking the ocean view from all the other houses here on the block, why such a house anyhow when all you've got is one adopted son who flunks summer school for nailing a shop-class hammer at the principal's nice daughter down the street's forehead, maybe now they'll just have to live on that boat, that *Winded Fever* of theirs they always got parked out in front, they must be out waterskiing the weekend away on, quite a welcome-back surprise, wouldn't you say, to come home to, and you think these winds will blow away all that grass seed we just seeded on our lawns?"

I saw my brother and his one-fence-over friend, Judd, walking across the field of ice plant the neighborhood pitched in to have planted as some sort of fire-stopping ivy that has leaves filled with sticky water we kids found lasted longer than any schoolyard chalk you rubbed onto the street to mark the lines for the sides of Nation Ball, New Kids versus Old Kids on the block, we got going every one of those summer nights. When I saw my brother and Judd walking across that field to where the blue swirl slide stood, I grabbed the nearest hamburger-greased hand of the kid next beside me on the blanket, who turned out to be the New Girl I had slammed flat-faced in Nation Ball the night before my parents kept on telling me to go over say you're sorry to have knocked her two front teeth out. I pulled the New Girl along by the hand with me across that snag-footed ice plant field with the sun straight up above in a cloudless sky, the winds getting the New Girl's unponytailed hair to go into her mouth as she yelled, "You jerk, cut it out!" Coming up on my brother and Judd, I saw the cone-shaped leftover from The Fourth fireworks in the back pockets of their cut-off shorts, and my brother and Judd, they both started to run that barebacked-boy run with feet kicking up at hindsides way ahead of me and the New Girl, who was stopping to tie her hair in a high-headed knot.

The New Girl rolled down her knee socks from her street-skidded knees and with a sorry-looking toothless grin said, "So you can throw a ball, so now let's see how you can run," and the New Girl, she took off, fast as she was, to skip-foot the sprinkler heads I got my feet all tripping in a bleeding way on as I caught up to where the New Girl stood at the poolside charcoaled cement patio like another big party barbecue had been going on with the barbecue grill turned upside down, its three legs sticking up, the domed lid off rocking in the wind, red-and-white striped cups floating capsized in the pool's ashed water, and the fanned-branch leaves of the one palm tree skimming along the pool's water where the winds pushed the leaves and a rubber sandal sole into a drifted pile against the tiled edge of the shallow-end steps.

"They're over there!" pointed the New Girl, to where my brother and Judd sat hunched on a black round table that from the middle had a pole going up with wires hooping out in the deep structure of umbrella, sending spidery sunshadows over the barebacked skin of my brother and Judd. The New Girl's knotted hair fountained in a spray behind as I followed her sneakered footprints, which cleared the ash to the table where my brother and Judd had the two Red Devils set up my brother was striking stick matches at that went out fast as they were lit under the cupped hands of Judd.

"Welcome to my palace," said Judd, when out of her sneaker the New Girl took the HAVE A SAFE 'N' SANE FOURTH lighter the neighbor, who went around claiming himself to be the son of the inventor of butane, had made up by the caseload and told us kids to put one in every mailbox, flag down, on the block if we wanted to get to stand on the roof of his three-story house to see the splattered fireworks shoot up the nighttime sky off all ocean boats way out beyond the canyon in the bay below.

The lighter had a built-in automatic windguard that flipped up when my brother hit the flame on HIGH—and when he set it to the unraveled wick, the Red Devil dudded sparkler-like off, nowhere near how at night far fires across the ocean bay lit the hills gold, the hills that under the sun gave out a gray rising cloud, making the sunsets that summer so large with color we kids would stop a losing Nation Ball game just for us to watch.

"Let me," said the New Girl, taking the last Red Devil, and said Judd, peeling the skin off the tops of his sun-fried ears, "I've got another house just like this one out in San Simeon," and "Let her," I said, "before she goes running home to her mother," and "She doesn't have a mother, all she's got is a hero of a fire-chief father, don't you, huh?" my brother said as he tossed the lighter to the New Girl, who turned and, one-handedly, "Yep," caught the lighter behind her back.

"Anyone care to join me for a dip?" said Judd, and kowa-bunga-ed a cannonball splash the wind threw over us as the New Girl covered the Red Devil with her I PASSED SUMMER SCHOOL T-SHIRT she had untied the sleeves of from over her hips, putting the Red Devil on the table top, setting the T-shirt over her head, saying, "This is how it's done."

Judd climbed the laddered high-dive shouting, "I am God!" loud enough to get the canyon's peacocks going off in their womanlike yelp the way they did every time the fire en-gines ran through the hills, making you lift the window shade or stand on the roof or turn around to your very own next-door neighbor's house to see how close the fire was or how far across the ocean bay our town's and the next town's over men had to go volunteering to try to put out what an entire county of town's men could not put out to stop.

The New Girl had her head shirted when my brother kneed her elbow to the hand holding the high-flame lighter and "Daddy!" screamed the New Girl, and shirt sleeves flapped away from her burning hair-knot as she belly-hit the pool water and "Banzai!" came Judd right onto her bobbing-targeted head.

Both Judd and the New Girl were down under the ash-stirred water when the wind sent the table onto its side and over us came the low-flying winged spread of peacock across the pool's waving waters, arcing to a bird-claw landing on the tip of the high-dive board where the peacock, feathered wings tucked closed behind the stretch of its neck, cried out into the wind carrying through the canyon. A hand holding a sneaker popped up from the water and then Judd's head and then the coughing face of the New Girl, her shirt bubbled up around her shoulders, her hair now short as my brother's cut short for summer boy-hair, as she armed the neck of Judd, who dog-paddled circles, shouting, "This is the life!" when across the

ice plant field I saw my parents, Judd's parents, the principal
with his baseball #1 SCHOOL IN THE COUNTY hat, and the Butane Neighbor Man with his foot-long cigar in his mouth,
running our way toward us kids.

"Act like you're dead!" my brother yelled, and arm-
hooked me down onto the patio cement, under the cooled-out
shade of the turned-over table, my brother's black-bottom feet
next to my face, and Judd pushed the New Girl over onto her
stomach, to float face down, same as he, and "Thanks for
inviting us," I heard my father say, and "Look, honey," said
Judd's mother, "a slide!" and "Quiet," said my mother,
"you'll wake the children!" as I heard the Butane Neighbor
Man scream "Geronimo!" into the pool and "Whee!" went
Judd's mother, shooting down off the slide into Judd and into
the New Girl, who were making their way out of the pool, up
the chrome laddered steps, and "Kids!" shouted the principal,
climbing the high-dive as the peacock glided down swoopingly
into the canyon of trees below. "Kids! Ever seen a flip swan
flop?!" and there went the principal, his hat flying off, ice
tumbling out from his tall glass of drink as he ran into the air
off the high-dive and "This is wonderful!" said my mother,
sitting on the cement at poolside, her feet kicking the water,
pouring one more from the jug into a red-and-white striped
cup she had gotten out of the shallow-end steps, and "I've
been looking all over for this!" Judd's father announced, slipping the rubber sandal sole onto his one-missing-sandaled
foot, and "What more could you ask for?" said the Butane
Neighbor Man, floating on his back, his sogged cigar in his
mouth as my father swam by him with a shark-attack finned-
hand cutting through the pool water's leaves and ash.

My brother, Judd, the New Girl, and I, we ran down into
the blowing smell of sagebrush, down mounds of dry dirt rock
rolling after us as we went jumping over fallen twisted trees
from last summer's fires, over plastic melted shields from winter's landslides, branches scratching at our bareskinned legs
and arms until we came to the man-made trail the fire trucks

ran on in the depth of canyon, the sun coming down on our months of beach-burnt skin, when the New Girl, her hair now wind-tossed shagged, said for us to "Watch!" as she flipped the pool-surviving lighter on HIGH and set the flame to the yellow grass that caught quick as hair to fire, and us kids, we took off, barefoot-slipping down the grass toward the blue slate of the always-there-waiting-for-us ocean, the hills across the bay giving off smoke clouds, the clouds we said were the Indian call to the Inland Winds, the faraway sound of sirening and the long-held yelps of peacocks in the onward rush of wind as we kids slid, pushed, shoved, ran with the all of what was left in the kid of us at the end of our lives that summer. Q

The Boys on Their Bicycles

EDITOR'S NOTE: *Eight years ago, William Shawn, then the editor of* THE NEW YORKER, *took a one-hundred-page section of Harold Brodkey's novel-in-progress,* PARTY OF ANIMALS, *and drew from those pages the piece that appears here. Despite Shawn's engagement with the work, the prospect of its publication in* THE NEW YORKER *was subsequently undone by a vote of the fiction editors overruling the editor. That version of that section of* PARTY OF ANIMALS *was then picked up by* THE PARIS REVIEW, *but did not run there either, this because George Plimpton, its editor, proved willing to put aside his claim in favor of an interest then being expressed by* VANITY FAIR, *which magazine, under the editorship of Richard Locke, had earlier declined the piece. But when Leo Lerman took over from Locke, the piece went back to* VANITY FAIR *at Lerman's request. Thereafter, however, Lerman was replaced by Tina Brown, whose fiction editor, Patricia Towers, invited Denis Donoghue to use the occasion to speak to his reading of Brodkey's work. It regrettably turned out—the vexatious matter of making room—that* VANITY FAIR *then found itself with too few pages to accommodate very much of the Shawn-Brodkey text. Accordingly, four excerpts were set, and these were then presented along with Donoghue's account of himself as a reader in lively attention to a literary enterprise of the very first magnitude. Which brings us to the following—eight years late—and all the more welcome for them.*

Take, for example, me and Jimmy Setchell.

Me at age almost fourteen, James S. the same, yet two grades behind, because of the month his birthday is in and because of my rushing my passage in school. We are American Jews, essentially undefined in the category of falling and ascending bodies.

Jimmy shouts, "Woo-hoo! Whoopsy-daisy . . ." We are on

bikes; the wind twists and edits syllables. The words sound odd and young. He wants to sound more grown up, and, so, in a tougher manner, he says, "Upsy-daisy . . ." That's no good; so, he persists, "Up we go . . ." Still not the way he wants to sound. He tries "Wowee," and "Geronimo-o-o." He thinks the last one is O.K. He smiles like a juvenile paratrooper and sails down a declivity and starts uphill.

I am looking out of my eyes at that moment. This moment. I am slouching in my biggish, skinny body at the edge of a weedy field of the whole moment.

I intended to end a remainder of innocence in me from my childhood that day. I intended to end my vow not to kill anything, or harm anyone, if God made things reasonably O.K. for my father—my father by adoption—who had been a youngish man, in his early forties then, and let him live for a while unterrorized and undespairing, not shamefully. That had been the grounds of the vow. Now my dad was dead, but that wasn't it: I was glad he was dead and probably wouldn't have done much to stop his death—this was five, nearly six years after the vow, which I had pretty much kept. It was that I was tired of the way I had been good; it had been a foul way to live. So, I intended to kill something in the course of the day. I had a disassembled .22, borrowed, extorted, from another boy. Jimmy carried it for me in a canvas pack on the bike rack in back of him.

Or I might decide not to kill. I might still refuse to kill. I might choose to remain solitary and pure, relatively undefended, even if that maneuver, of retreat, retreat inside my self, had gone so sour in the failures of the world and of my fathers that it had ruined the angle of the line of my inner fall—or ascent—for a long time. My desire now to use the rifle—well, I feel it as this thing that propels me toward life, perhaps fake, perhaps real, life. I proceed in a famine of companionship toward companionship. After my years as a child, I see companionship as a blood deed. I intend, today, to play with guns as a step toward acquiring social abundances and social knowledges. Let actuality begin—that kind of thing. Of the young man I was, it can be said, *he has an edge like a guillotine.*

This is meant to describe my mood, the killing something; and the question won't be resolved in this account.

I grin, I grimace as I pedal. I am very bookish. I name the non-transcendence, the non-thought of this excursion, *a day off,* a non-day, all real, nothing much, a day tilted (from the ordinarily moral and busy, from the sense of the future that is *not* secret). This is a form of private gaiety. My forehead and my mouth and my mind, my legs and my genitalia enter the next moment. I remember the sense of enlistment. I remember the brute intoxication of irrevocability.

I take the declivity and more or less shout, "Geron-i-m-o-o," too. Then I start pedaling furiously as I think I saw Jimmy do. My heart has trebled, quadrupled in the last year, and it is a new and noisy drum, a kind of smooth and then tormented engine. It startled me that I had new parts of myself, real sections, now. I hadn't had compartments as a kid.

My hands and wrists were new and big, my mouth was like a small salmon on my face, in looks and in how it felt to me: it leaped and spawned—words sometimes, sometimes expressions, in its excitements, in compulsions; a lot of my time then I lived in a chemical high, drugged, intent, and in chemical lows, furtive paranoias.

On a steep section, where the road lay as if sunken while it climbed between steep, shading rises of broken rock, with bushes and a lot of very skinny, very tall trees rising up on arched trunks well above me, here in the shady underworld, long after Jimmy starts angling on long diagonals while he pedals aloft, I continue straight to see if I am, as I half believe and would like to show, much stronger than he is and latently better at sports. The bike slows and goes yet slower. The bike locks onto the smudged rhythmlessness of making no headway. It's a little as if the front wheel is rotting or as if the bike is ploughing into an airy hedge. I persist. Breathless, then, partly defeated, I give in only the airy half-lurch before keeling (a fall), but I give in actively, heroically, more as if fighting back, me now the underdog—but mighty nonetheless. I right it, the bike; I grab the bike upright with my arms; I am leveraged on the straining arch of my body, my legs: calfless legs, handsome in their way, fairly strong but clumsy at the moment (my arms haven't much shape, either, but they're good-looking anyway—also—and strong), and I curse to mobilize myself. I threaten the hill with hell and God's wrath; the bike—its frame an edited, two dimensional diagram, lime green—is lifted (the front wheel comes off the ground); I aim it diagonally on the lesser slope, and then the galvanized half-leap and semi-glide forward means what I did was O.K. I am decently, skeletally athletic.

I then embark on the irresolute, crooked stitching back and forth, a tactic to get uphill farther; the bicycle occasionally lurches in a deadened, nerveless way.

Now, the morning swimmingly, sweatily jerks around in zigzags in front of my eyes, and I get postcard-like rectangles, road, roadside, ditch, fences, lawns, houses, window sashes, carriage lanterns, facades. The postcard rectangles, the pictured morning, is not looked at but indirectly seen and instantly remembered while I pedal and sweatily blink. It cuts and slaps paperishly at me. Behind my forehead, in my buzzing skull, my mind winces in steady, little slips. My legs do not pulse and bulge, though, and my eyes do not protrude, and my lips don't hang open as they did when I was small and went uphill on my bike, this bike; its seat is raised now.

I resented it that I had to remember in order to know what I saw, I have to put a step, a jackleg, a distance in, if I want to *know* what is in front of me. If I see alively, I sort of know, but I can't be sure.

The morning's crimped edges slap my inward eyes which are less shy because they see only when I blink or when the jackleg is in operation, when the corridors are patroled and speed is regulated—they are more elegantly mindful than my outward eyes.

I use my weight to force down the obstinate pedals, this one, that one, and they jerk up oppositely. The powering, or enabling, motto—the motto motor—is, *Get your ass up the hill.*

The light, the rays of the sun at a morning angle strike my eyes and then my wheeling ears and side of my neck as the bicycle slowly, heavily advances on an erratic line and switches directions again and then again. Flowers of glare flourish on my handlebars and on the spokes of Jimmy's bike. Jimmy is maybe sixteen yards ahead of me. I slouch more and more, becoming miniature in admission that I am clumsy, that I have certain deficiencies in my body and mind, omissions of experience and some muscular training and knowledge because of my father's having been ill and what was asked of me and that I am not gaining on Jimmy and am not a better athlete than he is—at this moment.

Everything in the world measures me and other men, and me against other men. I try to follow my duty. I try, also, as a mindly kid, to "know" what happens. That means to keep track, with a continuing sense, of what is done in the movement of time—that is, of what is actual. After a while, I remember too much and seem strange and bullying to some people—seem and am. Sometimes the abundance itself weighs me down, and this stuff crumbles into a pile, a single point or two, or indicators: *Here I am—sort of—sorry—this is a lousy hill.* At this time in my life I haven't the ability to phrase this and so it slides around like something unfastened in the trunk of a car, but I live it with an odd stubbornness.

Let me get up this goddamn hill.

I do the nut-thing of *maybe-it's-not-true that I'm here.* This shreds the brute intoxication of *irrevocability.* This destroys the fabric of the real—I mean, for me as audience of my own doings on this slope. My identity as an adolescent male, the space around my senses, titters now, and scowls in opposition to The Real: I'm a man, sort of, and I can do and think what I want: I'm not dependent like a woman or a child: I am and I'm not.

I start being in a school-y state, an agony, a restlessness, a reckless boredom: I am persecuted, deftly oppressed: *What kind of person* AM *I, why am I doing this, God. . . .*

I seek asylum as a brainy kid, I flee the country of such matters as maleness, and I think about books and soak myself in a pretense of rationality and escape the strain of bicycling.

At school, in order to pass as correct, since I won't risk being eccentric or having doctrines, I lie *always* and don't tell the teacher or the class when I make a book report or answer a question that a book or sentence or line in a poem is not the same for me on two successive readings, ever, the same sentence, the same *word—Don't be a philosopher; you tire everyone out, Wiley* (Wiley Silenowicz, Ulysses Silenus in a Jew-American version, since my adoption when I was two, when my real mother died). The second reading, which is meant to check the first, always so alters the snowy reaches of the first reading and my notes or impressions that it silences me: it's as if I was always wrong if I am right now. I hate myself because I lie about this and pretend I think it is mad stuff when I really think it is obvious and true, and basically useful. But I try to fit in even if at the expense of truth. *Don't tell people what you think; that's crazy.* So I don't. And I have daydreams of confessing someday to what I see. But I'm only a kid.

I am not A Good Kid with a single spine of doctrine and character. As I said, I have become *restless;* other people might say I started to get nervous—or they'd say Wiley's about to act up—again; he's mischievous, he likes to make trouble, he over-reacts. When I feel good, I don't judge things much except to say things like *These are people's lives, Let's be kind,* but when I'm bothered, like now, the neatened houses, wood and half-size brick, medium-strength dilutions of ideas of *farmhouses,* a prairie turned into cozy and self-conscious nooks, makes me embarrassed for everyone's life and for the sorrow in their lives and for the Middle West; and I know that would irritate a lot of people—I mean if they knew.

I don't understand, but I'm really unhappy suddenly, so I

call out to amuse and interest myself and to be a sport and to get back in touch with reality while I sweat and pump in the criss-cross pattern upward, "Hey, Juh—" (breath) "—IMMY."

My mood is uncured, and maybe worsened. This isn't felt as a smooth thing but lurchingly, among breaths and gasps. Anyway, the enlarged trees and shrubs of the lawns seem out of place in the Middle-western light, which is, after all, illumination for a prairie, for a vegetable sea, rising week by week in the summer, all summer long, a rippling broth of weeds and high grass and tall flowers, elbowing each other and leaning and bowing, culminating in sunflowers, farfetched and gargantuan, giraffe-like, maybe, August steeples, giant discs, solar, coarse, and yellow, nature's pragmatic and almost farcical climax before the collapse into autumn in a brown rush of cold.

The hill was once a burial mound. Now it's got these houses. The burial mound was once filthy, stinking—savages are no better than we are. Savages and everyone and everything else—each thing in the universe, with or without consciousness, has intent; a limitless will is a bloody tyrant-emperor—I mean, each thing tries to run everything, to have its way. Everything is imperial—without exception. Everything drags at you. This is a universe of trash tyrants. You have to sacrifice your life to prove goodness exists. *Do you think doing your duty sweetens things?* I sort of asked Jimmy in my head. Here's a secret: we are not entirely subject to laws. Everything can be cheated on for a while; you can put "an alternate irrevocability" into the system; you can *quickly* give something away, for instance, against your self-interest.

"Hey-ay, JUH-immy—YOU THINK GOODNESS egg-zisss(T)s?"

"Hunh?"

"YOU THUH-INK WE'RE IMPROOVING THE GAL-AX-EE?"

"WHA(T) Dyou WUHNNN(T) TO KNOW FORR?"

"I DON'T KNOW, I FORGOT, I'M OUT OF BREATH."

This is what I shouted, with various long pauses, or holes in the sound. But I wasn't exactly talking to him, and I wasn't quite talking to myself: it was an early adolescent version of weeping and sweating and being red faced.

"WE'RE ALL TIE-RUNTTS—" I know he won't get that: no one understands, no one listens through the technical haze of problems that inhere in speech.

As I pump, I feel an immoderate extent of will. I also get an erection, as I often do when I am in despair: this is a source of further despair. I go mad with sensual *restlessness*—a mode of despair; but even if I am to be a bad person in my life, I want to be it clearly and as *a disappointed good man,* do you know what I mean? When I feel the bike pedal scrape the macadam on one of my wobbly turns, I dismount. Good or bad, I am a free man.

I don't *want* to prove this in words, I don't want to lie. I don't want to argue anything; I want to *be* free. Now the neat lawns, the cretinous, *nice* houses (frightened, ill-educated), both decent and for sale—like new and still partly unconvinced whores—watch us. So does a weird-eyed nine-year-old girl who stares from the seat of a hydrocephalic plastic tricycle; the tricycle is bloated beyond my comprehension, a plastic machine.

"Hey, Woohiilee—Wha(t) suh—(y) udu wing?"

He switched syntax in midstream from something on the order of *What's the matter* to *What are you doing,* so there are a lot of alternate tones and possible sentences in his shout. I can read his noises, the bright, bent, burning wire hangers of syllabic shape: they're important noises, in a way.

The honest rejoinder which I make, almost absently, is "Duhwhuh?wuh(t) arR-(y)UuUw uhn-(eh)ee(ng)?" I indicate the last word because I want to say *simultaneously* (which shows interest and affection) "want," "doing," "saying," "shouting," et cetera.

I'm in cutoff Levi's, and I am shirtless. The road has a tar and tire and outdoor stink of a kind. My T-shirt is wrapped around the bar below the bicycle seat. Obviously, I ought not to unwrap it and wear it for what I think I am going to do. My eyes blink. I am half miserable. I don't *understand* what I am doing any more than I can *understand* at this point in my life why the houses along this road seem so decent and yearning to me at one minute and then boogied with ghosts and weirdness the next, and then itchy to my mind with a whisper of the wishes of the people who live there, their hopes about themselves, the long-extended efforts of their lives, some lives to be *good* within this framework of streets and houses, and then the houses seem like sly or communion-attending, love-armed and just about fully whorish the next. The same houses. Nuttily touching, then furtive, then merely things for sale.

"I'm a bondffi-i-er . . ." I shout: you can't shout *bonfire* and expect to be understood: it's too unlikely, unless you've been shouting about fires.

"Whun—di—(y)u ???uh?"

He's, oh, thirty yards away, uphill, half erased in glare.

We are so suburban, he and I, that we would not really shout even for a murder without blushing and other forms of embarrassment. We have been bribed (and browbeaten) into the low-voiced, self-important, figged-over, spear-pointing phalanx: we consider this the highest form of human manners and probably always will.

He is talking to me at a level almost of side-yard conversation, across the air, down the road, in this light, and with embarrassment because of the pretensions of the houses along this road, and because of the women in them, mothers, watching us maybe, judging us, judging our *manners.*

I say, "I'm waiting to see what I want to do. . . ."

What I said had a friendly charm, local but real; by local, I mean the way it was said, the way it was pronounced: *to a friend.* I assume he hears *charm*—male charm, likeability. He'll hear me the way he hears his brother, say; his brother is a well-known lecher in the local metropolitan suburban area. Jimmy's drawn to that stuff; so am I. He feels that such *charm*— if it works, of course—is power: You can always mock and try to blunt it or twist it away: or oppose to it your own *charm,* of whatever kind.

I sit down—lowering my bicycle as I go—and then I lie down, pretty much in the center of the road.

Now it is partly *charm,* like someone in a movie or a popular song demonstrating his *freedom,* and partly it is the gloomy act of God it was in my head to start with. Prone—and in despair—and palpitating with nerves and a kind of anguished belief in a number of things, and willing to accept meaninglessness-and-accident as final terms, sort of, out of an abundance of youthful kinds of strength, but still despairing, or at any rate, with a dark, even blackish hollowness inside me, a sense of palpitant emptiness, which is what I think other people mean when they say they are in despair.

So, then, here I am, with some printouts in my head about what I think I'm doing and why, with a basilica's nave of clarity of memory of me saying *I am waiting to see what I am going to do, I am waiting to see what I want to do,* and wanting turned out to be both a bleak and a nervously crowded thing and it all ended up here. Maybe it will turn into a joke, me lying in the suburban road, holding my bicycle in one hand by the handlebars, male in a so far spindly way.

I did not want to lie in the road. It's corny, it's dirty. I am fastidious and have intellectual pretensions (Middle Western, middle-class).

I reach over and unfasten my T-shirt from the bar.

Jimmy is a horrible person in a lot of ways—*a lot* of ways. Notice that he doesn't come rushing to see if I'm O.K.; he suspects a trap. He is buried in his own life; he has a lot of rebellious self-love. He sees me lying down and having a death-stroke or recovering or having a nervous breakdown; but he waits to see if it's safe to feel concern or even curiosity—will he be a fool if he offers to help, if he shows solicitude?—am I ribbing him?

I mind that because it interrupts the nobility of my effort to enact freedom and heartfeltness or something. Also *worship* of something—goodness, probably. Part of my purpose was that, and also to belong to the devil rather than to hypocritical pieties on this suburban road, et cetera. I think about Jimmy in a spasm of irritation and sadness: Why are middle-class kids so *canny*? The road stink rises around me; the tar gulpingly pushes against my knobby back. He doesn't trust me—my moods, my ideas and logics, arguments and beliefs. He lives with safe statements. He has only so many acceptable signals of peace and aid in his data bank. He is about as much a romantic adventurer in thoughts and words about love and help as your average Boy Scout troopmaster.

I lay my bike on the macadam: it had no kickstand, and I still held its handlebars. I loathe lying in the road. I loathe most of the would-be *important* acts and big-time gestures I make. I loathe being imprisoned in things I start. So, I sit up and put on my shirt and I fold my legs in a lotus posture: then I unfold them and sit like that on the tarry surface.

The nine-year-old girl and her shrewd and good-looking and slim-titted and cretinously sweet and suspicious mother are holding each other's hands and watching *me*.

Maybe they're worried about me, both ways, as a possible menace and as someone who is to be worried about because he has to be helped soon if you want to be a *nice* person about it.

Jimmy coasts crossways across the road and down a bluff.

My mood is an encampment of an army. He's a mere Carthaginian—no: Gaul.

"Jimmy, where are we headed?" I say. "What does my life mean?" He ignores that, or I say it too blurredly and he can't figure it out; it's too unfocused.

He is nearer but still cautiously yards away. He glides on his bike, mostly backward, brakes with his feet, looks at me, looks at the sky, hesitates. How does someone who is not a truth-teller recognize a truth? He never knows why I'm irritable. He thinks I'm strange.

My sense of action, me being a man(ettino) of action, that fades, and my mind resumes its privacy because Jimmy is so suspicious of me. My images are resummoned; they return mostly as fumes of will, they never stay the same for long, but outdoors that changeability is worse, is even foul—although beautiful. To claim otherwise is to lie. To be an invalid and kept indoors is intellectually more honorable. For example, the reasons and mood I had are gone, and I don't any longer know why I'm sitting on this macadam in humid, smoggy sunlight, in my shorts and T-shirt. I am now martyred by carrying on an act of will that once had a warbonnetted ferocity (and freshness) to it; I have compromised it a dozen times by now; the whole thing is dull and stinking; it's time to give up, stand up, but that idea (of standing up) becomes sad, an infliction. The macadam stinks and sticks; pebbles gnaw into my thin-muscled butt and the skimpy calves of my legs; the idea of freedom has turned into an outline, penciled and geometrical, which may be colored in, or painted, and then seen as containing *life*—that's a symbol. Mostly. My existence plunges and filters and buzzes along *meanwhile;* but I am a prisoner of the drawing, and my life is, too. I mean I believe in freedom even if it's only the posture one takes for the fall.

He's looking at me: I have the sense, maybe wrong, that he's *amused. Charmed,* in a way. That's not O.K. It's distracting. The landscape, the slope, the wall and tree, the staring women, James, my companion up to a point, everything is sun-capped above abysses of the hardly seen *truth* of a gesture, let alone of my works and days. This matches, or simulates, the visual truth, which is that what I see flimmers over or at the rim of abysses: the *hardly seen by me*—literally *half* seen. I see in fits and starts, with emphasis here and there—near abysses of shadows and subsidiary glimmers. *The periphery.* The at-the-moment Minor Stuff—in which truth might be found. It is the case that I see one thing—Jimmy's mouth, let's say—and I hope the rest is there.

I now rise and am half on one knee, undecided about everything; one hand is on the macadam.

My mouth feels like a salmon, muscular, tugged; Jimmy's mouth, now seen in this light and at a distance when he turns his head to me, I see as a large dot, or maybe big dash on his face, but it is remembered, imagined, as a mouth with shapes and colors seen in another light and at different angles; it is as free as a particle in the wind, it seems.

I lay on my bike on the macadam: it had no kickstand, and I still held its handlebars. I ganglingly collapse backward, because freedom also means not caring if I break my back or my neck, sort of. I lie panting. Jimmy is now nearer, near enough so that I am released from the Roman camp of a kind of solitude; I am unlocked from my head and am aware, or even oppressed, by him, his presence; I can see that he glimpses me and disbelieves; that is, he only partly believes I am doing what I am doing. He now coasts backward some more, on the diagonal, back down the slope, toward me, to the body of glimmer and shadows and odd behavior that is me. Who is me. Whatever. He halts, his legs spread, the bike heroically between his thighs. On my shirted back, the tar is a bed of cupping, sucking, semi-melted octopus tentacles, fatally attached.

I am in a sort of rage of thwarted gesture and I want him to "love" and admire me. To love and to admire are so overlapping, they are just about the same emotion in me, separated by one or two seconds of mental time, seconds in which I blink and compete and do my best with the pain of admiration and try to fit it. I am heartsick but stubborn inside my lying here, and I am lonely because this thing I'm doing seems like metaphysical brattishness pretty much—not entirely—but I want him somehow to help this stuff along until it's O.K. It occurs to me that one has to devote almost a lifetime to this kind of act (and thought) to make it grown-up and really good (valid). I ought to go limp now and be married to this and really suffer. Only pain can validate this, can validate me, and this is hell to know, to guess at, I mean, and to live out.

It is bratty, therefore, even if it's honest of me, to want Jimmy to help—but I insist on being *happy sometimes*. And Jimmy can make me happy(er). But it is facile and glib not to suffer in one's truths, they are real acts, and strain the shit out of you in your real moments, and it's dumb not to recognize that they are true. But it's facile and glib to suffer all the time; things can turn good without warning, without any warning at all.

I said, moist-eyed, "I am a free man—boy—man." Then I said, in a very well-educated way but mumbling and local, "It is one of my privileges not to have to be careful to make sense by your standards when I speak."

I want him to remember that I'm a smart kid and can be—well, *trusted,* you know. So, I had spoken in a really careful sentence. To show I could be trusted—this was out of loneliness, and folly, a cheating on myself, to explain myself as if in a footnote in school. I mean, I heard dialogue in my head— him saying, *Wiley, what are you doing? What are you saying? Why are you showing off? Are you being a jackass?* I saw this on his face—in his eyes, outlined and bowed and pointy, and in the set of his mouth, and I answered it in the long and careful sentence, which he hardly heard. He thought about it and then dropped the effort of remembering and figuring out so many words.

"Wiley, what is it?" he said—as if I'd groaned and not spoken.

It was much more tender than I had expected.

I'd finessed him into it, I'd willed it, but part of the point was also what he decided on when he came near me.

Then he said, "Are you all right?"

"I am—a—free—man."

"Did you have an asthma attack?"

He wasn't being pleasant. I mean, who wants *medical* attention?

He wasn't being derisive—just bored and standoffish and self-enraptured in his concern.

"Listen, jackass, I don't believe in manliness," I said.

Of course, he didn't know *the context,* so that didn't make too much sense.

Jimmy blinked: "Why are you attacking me—now?"

"Oh, cut the innocent bystander crap." Then I said, "*You* exist, you do things for people, jackass—my feelings about *human* freedom don't make *me* a jackass, Setchell, whatever you want to think—for your own purposes."

I add metaphysical overtones to his sense of his own day while he gets along in his canny goings-on.

When I talk, the stuff I'm saying grinds into me as failure and loneliness.

I am falling, in a state of off-again, on-again, blurred, low-key rage for freedom, or whatever it is; and his looking at me, in whatever degree of affection or mix-up or incuriosity or desire or whatever state and mixtures of things he's in, doesn't help—the light is behind him, the pale sky; and he's like the dark nucleus at the center.

We are shirtless and barelegged, bareankled: I'm in running shoes; he has bicycle shoes.

I can understand his not understanding me when I talk. I'm not a clear person.

He twitches; he isn't calm, and, so, when I see that, I get ashamed in case I've been a show-off and have upset him; but, really, you know, I don't know why he twitches, and, in a way, I am too cowardly to ask, but his life is attached to mine today, for these hours; I'm immune to nothing.

I am not tough—merely mean at times. I stand up in quick stages, *segments*. I haul my bike upright.

Then he reached over, and I was careful not to stiffen, and he touched me with two fingers on the back of my neck where my hair started and he picked off a piece of tar. The tar was stuck to me, and then it whistled free; and behind it, on my skin, was a burning sensation, insecurely placed, but it did abut on an emotion.

His fingers moved in what I considered to be a Jimmylike way, like the words in a first-grade reader, careful and clear, so that you don't get startled by meanings.

But I get startled by them anyway. I am a glorious mirror for other people in some ways, unfortunately—for their heroisms of existing in the real world. I often feel I don't exist physically, in the inherited world of parents and the like. Sometimes it's O.K. I stood still, and he went after some of the pebbles that were stuck to my back under the loose T-shirt again; I have a skinny back. It's odd not to be someone worthless. I grew stilled inwardly, pondlike, *girlish*—I mean with guilt and responsiveness. I really mean with greed and also with a kind of suspicion, and then with stiff gratitude, stiff with resistance because of the suspicion, and then not, but kind of wildly generous, like a kid, but one my size—me, I guess. His fingers are *small,* considering his size. I'm six-two and he's six-three. His fingers taper down and are kidlike in the last joints. "You're being so goddamn tender, I can't stand it," I said, and he gasped, or groaned, like my dad—as my dad used to, wanting me not to talk. I would guess the tenderness was real, but it's his and I don't know what it means in relation to who I am and what I do and what I have just done. I was overborne by the mysterious chemical fires he lit with his acting like this and his continuing to act—with tenderness—while currying me of dirt after my dumb gesture, or whatever I should call it. What I'm trying to get to is to say that this stuff with the fingers, the tender-fingers business, occurs along the lines of the irrevocable, too—the masculine irrevocable.

If he likes me this much, why didn't he lie down beside me?

Why didn't he say, *Jesus God, Jesus God?*

How come he's so stubbornly set on doing things his way, inside his own way, inside his own life?

Why didn't he give up his own will and his own speech? Look, he's being so—*nice.* Medically generous. In each touch, in each movement of his fingers are inspired little puffs of soul-deeps and absent-mindedness, like birds in dust or leaves forgetting themselves and leaning or fluffing and being almost still: stilled birds in very early morning sunlight. Something like that.

How can I live up to his silly goddamn fingers?

How do you live up to anything halfway decent?

How do you live with anything that's really just about entirely decent?

People don't stay decent. This is a trap, what he's doing.

It's so terrible to be irritated by people. How do you live with people?

The tenderness was already turning nasty. His fingers were getting sharp and quick and gougey. Of course, it wouldn't stay like that, either, but now his touches were rough and rebuking.

Then he began doing it as if I was inanimate and my back was his teddy bear or his bike tire; that was O.K., but then it's not O.K. Frankly, I am not usually in love with him—only a few moments here and there—but I had been for a few seconds: paralyzed, frozen, stilled, or whatever, for a moment there.

If he'd been knowingly *physical*, limitlessly sexual by a sort of nostalgic implication back toward childhood but with self-conscious purposes and within virginal limits and virginal and whorey knowledges, like a smart kid, it would have been easier. Different. Well, to tell the truth, he was like that, too, but slyly, and with more vanity than confidence. Second by second, he changed, or I saw or imagined a change. Some of what he did was derisory. Also, I hate being touched.

Finally, I pulled away from him, glanced at him. I suppose he thought it was all nuts, but I kept thinking I was being obvious and that he understood everything—*every single thing.* And he did, in his way. After all, I am obvious in what I do and very, very *logical.*

All over my back and my mind—my consciousness, my feelings—are his fingers, and the tones, and senses of possibility and of other stuff, little raw, alive places, not necessarily sane stuff—maybe just kid stuff. I put my bike's handlebars in his hand—a sort of comic act, a sort of *Here's a toy for you. Isn't life disgusting?* And I glanced at him knowingly, with rebuke. But he's not likely to get it; he didn't remember *he'd* been rebuking; he never did remember things like that. And then, because I didn't want to do what I did next—that's first; and, second, because the comic thing drove me now, and all the wounded or whispery places, which are growing shabby and vague mostly, but are also burning brighter; and third, because I did love him, *maybe,* and didn't love myself yet in my rather handsome adolescence but was learning to by using him; and his feelings about me; and fourth, because it excited me not to *understand* this stuff, I lay down in the road again.

Now, he and I could observe the act of *a free man*—so to speak—a second time, and maybe it had gone null and wasn't dangerous anymore, unless, of course, he did understand and would somehow prop me up in being me and doing this, and then it would blaze up, the act and us, masculinity and meaning, maybe men in love, who knows what.

So I did it.

So I am supine and I say, "See—I am a free man—*boy*—*man.*"

The last part was just an automatic memory thing.

He said, "You want me to take the pebbles off—or not(tt)?" He was still in the earlier phase, his feelings were still back there; I guess I can say that—and me being supine on the tar now, again was more an interruption than the next step along the line of *irrevocability*—and what not. The multiple *t* when he ended *not,* made his mouth into an ugly grimace: this means he is irked, bored, not watching me now, not going along with *it*—whatever *it* was.

"The joke went flat?"

I'm lying there and looking up at him—the tar feels lousy.

"What joke?"

I can't explain, since I mean and don't mean *joke,* so I say, "Unnhawwahh"—an expressive noise, maybe exhortatory as well as evasive. I mean it's unclear—but expressive.

Long pause. Then he says, "I don't think you have a good sense of humor, Wiley." (*"Wu-high-ly."*)

I turned my face to the side, cheek to the pavement. "I get told that a lot," I said, from my mouth and eyes down there alongside the pavement.

I felt lousy and coerced by the near-kiss of the tar and the *meaning* of me doing one thing and Jimmy not following, so that if I persisted in it it would have some other meaning that I wasn't too sure I wanted; if meaning is a place, it was a place I didn't want to go to, a weird planet with a bad reputation. So, I heaved myself up again quickly and said, "See, I get sick and tired, and fed up *too*. I'm through with half-assed gestures, O.K.? Now, will you please pick the goddamn crap off my back, and don't pinch, and don't take forever—"

I offered him my back. It's like a half-assed order; you try to get away with this thing; or you're asking—with some embarrassment, I guess—for some of the tenderness crap. Jesus, I figured it was clear I was getting even for his saying that about my not having any humor.

My voice stayed deep, which is a good sign that I'm getting somewhere in my life in general: I'm learning to pitch my voice like a grown-up.

Then his tenderness, which was flickering like leaves, became knowing and sad, and he shoved my shoulder—because I was *moody*—with a hard shove of his hand. It is not quite credible in some ways, considering my lousy life, but I am spoiled and very handsome (sort of)—and he shoved me to show *his* freedom, but it was truncated as a gesture of ownership or courtship or what not. The style, the tone of it. Things showed in it. One thing that showed was that he was afraid of me.

He was a sad boy but we weren't at a sad age. I said, "You probably have more free will than I do because you get along with your mother." I also said, "I always seem too planned out to myself; I have a lot of very pseudo-carelessness about free will."

He was *knocking* some crud off the knobby part of my back—i.e., the spine—and part of the upper muscular cape too. Up close and speaking either turned away or close to him, I felt the syllables to be like hollow tubes or like near-kisses; their shapes are all weird and *segmented*. When I said *pseudo*, I turned toward him to help make sure he'd get it, that he'd recognize the word. I look at his eyes but I can't see that he does hear. So, I turn away so that when I say *carelessness*, it goes shooting off like a stalk into the air away from him.

I usually felt he wanted me to explain myself to him, and when I did, he didn't always listen—that is part of my dislike for him. Usually, he *wasn't* listening. If he didn't listen, he didn't have to judge and change mentally if I was true or interesting. If he wasn't going to change mentally, then not enough was at stake for things to be exciting and real for us. For me. I mean, change in step with each other rather than alone and somberly: it was exciting to be in step, and so on. I hate to change all by myself: you know it's going to be lonely, it's going to be bad. You just rattle around then, you have no coordinates to measure sanity by; it seems inhuman. He had that stubborn virgin's thing of undercutting the moments by making them into things that didn't matter, since nothing really happens ever. The virgin's lie.

If you notice everything, you won't like anyone—I'd been told that a lot.

Notice everything: that's rich. I ignore most of what I notice, like everyone else.

The extraordinary truth, so anguishing to me, of the reality of life as fires of passion, within the moments, and only barely referred to in the fluster of acts involved in our flirting with such big questions as whether to be really loyal to one another—all that stuff is ungraspable to me, but I feel comprehension always near, so help me—I swear this is how we lived. To live almost with virtue instead of with a grinding shrewdness, it's just beyond thought, and then, as I said, the comprehension hangs around and seems very close—in tenderness stuff mostly, when it's mixed with a little or a lot of some kinds of violence of meaning, when you're not cold and selfish but seem to be careless with yourself. Extravagant, wonderful. A fool. The comprehension always seems as if it will get clearer, that history will explain it or bring it, that I'll find out about this stuff when I get older. I sometimes want to rush things.

I don't want the fixed kind of comprehension, which is so satisfying, but the other kind, which is a sort of response and loss of everything but the response in the flicker, in the exploding novas of the moments, of the new turns one's history is taking in (pardon me) love for one another.

The comprehension that comes is about living out the stuff involved in belonging to someone. Anyway, when you're in the middle of loving, then that incomprehensible comprehension which is so dangerous and fine and never entirely apt is ballooning in your breath and eyes and chest just about all the time for a while but erratically. Even without that, I feel, and have since infancy, that we are pregnant with each other's lives, every minute, anyway, with how someone feels and does in the world, and this tends to fill me with love foolishly sometimes and makes me obnoxiously gay and sort of all right, no matter what. I deal in unnecessary amounts of everyone's happiness—happiness-in-the-concentration-camp is how my ill parents and I lived for years at times, between not getting along and being horrible, of course. So, when I'm talking to anyone I don't feel merely sorry for or put off by badly—and even then, too, if I'm honest—I have his or her happiness in me, his or her life, and he or she has mine, in him, and they blast you or do you some good.

The necessity I feel and have for the impossible return, the approximate recurrence, of certain smoky moments, images that arise only in this person's or that person's company, what does that mean? I take that to be what I mean by love. Here we are, this is us with each other now, and we have this queer amalgam of trust, treachery, tyranny, chemistry, and truce, and the seductions of language; and we have here, also, the paltry allegiances of our *friendship* short of *love,* short of admitting slavishly that there is *necessity* in our experiencing images and reality together, him and me, side by side, in each other's company. I live like that, but I don't really like it—maybe it's sort of an irrevocable kind of agonized and ecstatic flirtation

with happiness. I cannot bear this. An ease in our being together is almost a reward of a successful sidestepping of affection—I saw it like that, too. I felt it. I came to experience a kind
of death I was so overloaded with the moment's reality. I
choked on it, the stoniness and wilderness, and the ocean and
fields of *possibility* of the reality of emotion. I felt a kind of
earnest despair at being without such emotion except in spurts
when it is begotten by our courage in being—oh—attractive to
each other—our courage cohabits with impossibility. Impossibility is a funny term. We are a disobedient and surprisingly
successful species. I don't know. Maybe that's just American
romanticism, you know?

In the landscape of neat houses, of love and beauty as
locally understood, among the cruelties and famines of that
stuff, a lilac hedge is visible in a yard nearby. The moment is
fleeting (as hell). I am not able to grasp or bear anything. I am
as capricious and as tense as if I were a beautiful horse or a
beautiful boy, which in a way, for a while, I am. My middle-
class stupidities and gracelessness goad me. I say, "Leave that
filth on my back; I like it; it's a badge; you take too goddamn
long; you have the fingers of a butcher."

He stopped—his fingers abandoned my skin. My theory is
he was relieved. He felt love as a tragic burden or as suffoca-
tion—*felt it* means he didn't have to say it in words: he could
"know it" and let it go at that. Anyway, it's only a theory.

I hold back from Jimmy not because I'm clever and shrewd
about people or anything but because he fits over my senses
and my mind in a way I don't want. I don't want to be more
like him or more him than I already am.

See, I've gotten away from the act of loving him by a set
of pretty simple steps.

He said, "You're careless." Meaning *reckless*. He said,
"You didn't prove anything." Which means, What good is the
glamour of you acting up and having my attention like this?

He is weak in a number of ways.

I am choking as in surf when you swallow salt water. I love

and don't love in a kind of rucking up of attention and voice—I mean it's a sudden wrinkling up and gathering together—unless I am being soft and seductive and *reasonable,* as I am with women, going along a predetermined path so that a woman inside her physical and other differences can know where I am, and not be blinded, and doesn't have to be over-poweringly shrewd and deductive—i.e., conventional, knowing about things outside herself in a handy way, inspired smally: I'd like to say it like that—but can figure me out and choose me if she wants.

I don't think anything else works with women, they're so stubborn.

I said, "You hope. You wouldn't know what I proved even if it kicked you in the head."

He's hurt, numbly: "Wuh-huh-*i*-lee . . ." The protest is unbelievably vague in detail but it's clear as a threat: Obey these vague laws, avoid these vaguely worded, maybe *immense* punishments that lie in my unhappiness OR ELSE. . . .

I say coldly, in careful syllables, "You have no noticeable brain yet." It isn't true, but he isn't sure, and he suffers as if it were true. His eyes get weird.

Before that starts to make me sad and maybe really guilty I say, "You're merely very, very good-looking." That's like a joke; that's to cheer him up. But at first he suffers from the denial of his mind that seems to be, and then the praise settles in, and his eyes loosen up. Some.

As for me, what settles into me is a sense of my being a puppet, moved around by semi-automatic earlier decisions, such as to be polite, or politic, or whatever. Whatever it is, I'm not free with people, free to risk things, free toward their vulnerabilities, their rights. I'm less freed or free than a stubborn girl is. Me having a bad temper and not too many friends is a sign of my being trapped like that and getting free from people even if it is lonely. . . . It's also a sign of this, that often people like me more than I like them. Well, tough shit . . . So, in order to be free, I say, in a very independent, unmaneuvered, unquick, unquickened, *nice* voice—I do this morally; I am free to be ethical if I want—"It's not true that you have no noticeable brain yet. Your brain is very noticeable—"

Now he says to me, "Oh, man, you really are a Jekyll and a Hyde."

He doesn't mean really two characters in one skin; he means more than that: one part of what he means is that I am a quick-change artist who is also someone cruel who subsides from time to time into kindness—into flattery.

"You know I like you, you know I think you have a mind. You know I think it's good to be around you when you're talkative. You can be a hell of a civilized guy."

I think he is basically, humanly *hurt* inside, no matter what happens.

Friendship is what we're here for; I said, "It's good to be around you. You're civilized."

"I'm very careful about my manners. I think I know how to act." He said this pleasedly—also like a scientist reporting on it.

"Is that why you take such long pauses between speeches? Are you figuring out what to do?"

"Cut it out," he said in pain—maybe threateningly, too.

He has no real wish for honesty, which also surprises me and makes me somewhat bored, some. His mother and his brother and his father probably picked on him for being slow in conversation. Calculating is what it amounted to, unalive: he didn't have a whole hell of a lot of spontaneity or honesty or improvisation in him.

We really didn't understand each other's really personal diction.

Well, I was tired of what was happening, I was antsy, nerved up from the exchange, and I wanted another venue of reality, one of less speech, less of things being tricky—I mean, there's more than one way to be laconic—and so I started to remount my bike.

"I proved a lot of things," I said, as I did it, remounted my bike. "I mean, by the way, you'd see I proved some things if you would choose to use your civilized mind."

"Oh, uh, Wuh-hi-i-lee, were you setting a trap?"

That is, did I flatter him (I thought he was saying this, something like this) and then watch to see if he was egocentric? And not a good guy?

I hadn't pedaled, only kicked the pavement, and, now, wobblingly, I slowed and stopped again.

I stood and faced him. Stood? I'm mostly on the bike and wobbling back and forth, forward and back. "No, I wasn't. I make up stuff as I go along. I'm just saying to you I proved *a lot of things.* Lying in the road proved a lot of—oh, Christ."

He'd gotten me to start to try to explain; explanations are demeaning: you're in service to the other's understanding you then; you're not allowed to live but have to stand in a clear light and just explain. *He'd* set a trap. It was his system: he'd got me off guard by accusing me of what he was about to do and then I went into being naive to prove him wrong. Now he's deadpan but it's as if he's grinning.

I have one leg over the bar of the bike. "Are you grinning?"

He's all covered with glare, and shakes his head, or I imagine it, because he is deadpan insofar as one approximately makes this stuff out in real life, in real light.

He's listening carefully; he's looking at me. I snoot him. I scratch my back, contortedly, more and more furiously.

"You goddamn mind hater," I say mildly from within my contortion, absently; but I mind the way he is, I hate and loathe him, pretty much, but, of course, I don't know *for sure* that he set a trap unless he tells me so.

"Wiley." The inflection means *cut it out;* but that wasn't enough: he said, in a further convulsion of hurt, or whatever, but that is really anger in him, *"Cut it out."* His anger isn't like mine; he *says* things that have to do with anger: anger silences me. He threatens to *hate* me actively for a while—that's what *cut it out* means if you haven't got real authority. He knows I hate him now, finally, but he wants to finesse me out of it. I mean he wants to *browbeat* me out of it and not change and listen to me or be sympathetic.

He has no gift of prophecy about emotional things, and his anger doesn't suggest to him a lifetime of guilt and grief or give him any hint that he is attempting to imprison me in praising him to balance whatever admiration or desire he feels toward me—or toward my *methods*, or my abilities—or his desire to experience the way people treat me. . . . He wants to have my life be his, sort of. That's love.

Competition—and curiosity—are always in it.

Anger for him, since he's slow and as if not conscious when he feels it, is merely release as justice. It's a happy ending but a little way back before it's *proved*, if you follow me. . . .

I stopped scratching my back and started pedaling and was surprised and hurt after a few seconds that we were on a hill still. I would shortly be out of breath. "This goddamn hill—is *endless*—" And I used his name in its most formal version: "James."

He'd caught up to me on his bike and he was being over-sized, self-consciously even huge—and athletic—just on my right, shading me, overshadowing me: this is a form of black-mail—and also of physical threat—and that, plus more, makes it comforting to him, or useful, or whatever. He is a marvel of power and reason and being *athletic* and of winning-out-in-*his*-way.

I said, "You remember one thing: Hurt me and you'd better kill me, because if I survive I'll smash you to bits some-day, if it's the last thing I do. Get me? Think about it or you'll get very, very *hurt*." Now he's pulling ahead of me. I said, "Don't threaten me. We've got a whole *day* of this crap ahead of us." Then more nicely, sort of more nicely, "Why is—does *friendship*—"I had changed the form. I often did. Verbs are sick things anyway—they're so general; think of all the ways people walk and how differently different people and in what different ways, according to their states and moods, all of that, they do walk; and then think of the word *walk* but then think of it as you usually think of it, as just meaning *not run* or whatever or something even more vague and general: it's sick.—"Why is— does *friendship*—always have this quarreling crap in it? Do you think maybe we're vulgar? Is it different for Christians, you think?"

He wasn't listening.

He's maybe ten yards ahead and pulling away.

Actually, he hears, but in a way that's complex. Not only are we on bikes and moving, so that the air draws out and dilutes syllables and makes thickets in which they get lost, but he's also a wretched and solitary victim now, and he doesn't *have* to listen—except to plots against his throne. Nothing else is as interesting to him just now.

So, I feel the way he's listening is not real, which means it's not acceptable to me.

But it's O.K. We're young. We have a lot of energy.

So, I'm ready, I can go on, I know Jimmy has gotten set to fight—vaguely but violently—both inside and outside his usual tactics, family tactics (his family's), and also inside and outside of *loving* me, or whatever the emotion should be called. He doesn't like loving people, or me, the one he chose, although I helped and didn't exactly drive him away all that much, as I do some people.

He said—he is more or less not seated on his bike but is pedaling from a half-erect posture, powerfully—he more or less shouted, "You be reasonable."

Leave his maybe ridiculous superiority alone, he means.

His tone says that he belongs to me in a way but that I have to die into a role if I want *his* devotion (such as it is), with him in the lead, et cetera. . . .

I get scared because I can't afford to hate the day or him: I'm in somewhat desperate circumstances about my life, about enjoying myself sometimes *when I get the chance.* My home life is poor. It's a home death at my house.

Say something PLEASANT. Go to the bins in your head where

words and phrases of a business order of things, which have to be *comprehended* in a much-trafficked way, fairly steadily, are kept, and use those in a businesslike way to make the kind of talk that rests palely in the head in a business part of the world. My head is the norm, or whatever. Get some polite formulas. Use sensual stuff unsensually to cut down the consequences; this is social wit, this is *sensible*—you take meaning away from what is sensible to the senses—what you see and feel in local areas of the real that muffles things and keeps them safe and sound.

Sort of.

Maybe.

I say, "This hill is eight hundred thousand goddamn meters long—straight up. Maybe that's why flat, desert landscapes are more religious. They don't wear you out with a lot of tiring, up-and-down crap. You project the end, and it makes sense then—Hey, cheer me up: we know this is not a Himalayan Alp, right?"

Jimmy is bicycling well ahead of me, but now, as I say those things, shout them really, and joke, he slows until his rear tire is beside my front one. The road is empty except for us on this part of the grade. "There's a lot of religion in the Himalayas— I heard about it," he says, turning his head back and forth to let the words flow back to me. He is giving me this; conversationally he is giving in and being nice.

But he is also manipulating and being bossy; he is correcting my stuff and making everything from his point of view rather than listening to me; he is removing the point of what I said, and aiming the talk in another, more of a travelogue direction. But he's also being *friendly*.

"But this isn't limitless like that," I say—I'm in *his* conversation now.

I don't want to talk to the power manipulator he is—he lives in a world of no settled formality; that's what his nonmemory and the comparative *stupidity* are for: bossiness, tyranny, an absence from the duties in being with someone—but

I don't have a choice of anyone else for the day now—unless I want to give up on the day.

So I say, "Well, yes, but the road does have *this slant,* this godforsaken slant—" But I have a private rule of not talking to myself and of not laughing at anybody, so I said to him, to be useful and to add a little rhetorical and pious class to the day, "God's shepherding meaning is gone"—I say this in a mumble and he knows I am laughing at him, but I am defeated and will behave because of what I did earlier and I'm not *a big winner* anyway. . . . I don't do the thing of showing my shoulder holster all the time or mentioning my armies and saying *Watch it;* I'm demonic and sweet both; I let who I'm with have free will and undergo condemnation by various tribunals in them and in me. I can sort of get along and even be at home, queasily, in the eerie and tilted and nervous democracy of others' claims.

Hard politics, the politics of happy, happy charm.

I have renounced my vow and will prove today I don't fear God or hell.

I stand and pedal. My left side happens to be in shade, cooler, partly colored black at the jogged periphery of my rainbowy (salt-prismed) vision. Jimmy is risen in his bike saddle, too.

God, we're tall, immense shadow-throwers.

He asked me to do this today—come riding. I am here for his purposes, after all—I mean, on the basis of invitations.

(My mother said, *For how long do you plan to be gone from here?* She's ill: she has cancer.)

The moist, sweaty soil of *shadows* on my left side gives way at the suburban hilltop to sun on that side as the road turns west and my face is faintly veiled in its own flowing shadows now for the first time in a while.

The queer mumble of noises, noises from the valley, at this considerable height, none of the noises distinct, are like sounds in a mechanical underbrush. The noises are dimmed, partly smothered in the fat, polluted air.

Meaninglessness is in devoting one's attention to the noises after they are identified and judged as ugly.

"Look hard at the day and judge God, look hard and lose sight of God—how about that?"

"Yeah? I don't know. What do you mean—Wiley?"

I'm not sure we knew his *superiority* was gone. Maybe it was a truce.

"I may be quoting. I don't know. If you look hard, you get political—that's all I meant. Detail means God is not there—that's all. I prefer the details to God: that's by the way, by the way."

"Yeah? I don't know, I don't know that I think you're right on that."

He's holding onto the crown with both hands.

"I don't have to be right. You do: you have to make more sense than I do. I have a reputation. I've proved I know what I'm talking about sometimes. I can afford to be unclear. . . ."

"That's true." Then: "Wiley, why do you attack me all the time?"

"You had the upper hand for a while."

"You never let anybody have the upper hand."

"Jesus, you're so full of Krap with a K it makes me vom-itttt—"

"Cut it out, Wiley."

In boyish shame at the imperfections of my speeches and my affections, my mind opens onto the morning. I am looking down over my arms, my hands, the handlebars of the bike, past the racer's wheel in motion, to the road spinning or pulling, or being pulled backward under the wheel.

After a second or two, the slope picks up steepness going down.

I enter what is like a tunnel, windy and speedy, going downhill in an accelerating swoop and with half circles of rush pulling at my hair. The increment of speed and the steadiness of balance form transparent tents and invisible hallways and domes with echoes in them.

And something like the hands, fingers, tongues, feet, and toes of the wind push and prod me in an airy but semi-breathless tumble, a kiddy free-for-all, a seduction in the key of free fall, and weirdly roofed and walled, I guess, in the concentration or seduction of the senses or whatever it is, in staying alive and whizzing dangerously down and down and down. . . .

I am startled by how pretty sometimes the musics of movement are.

Jimmy idly—or as if idly—passes me.

He can't see me anymore; he is ahead of me.

The animal sense of the moment tickles, it startles in a blood way—I glance up with a fox's heat of dreadful attention, a predator's study in the wanton speed, the early feverishness, the being out for the day with James Setchell (Jimmy), the irregular heat of the morning, aliveness, the downhill, the riding no-hands, the idle whooping under my breath, air on my bare chest, skinny ribs, and with my face upturned I catch sight of a wide-winged hawk; it swings hangingly in the air not far past some trees, not far, not high, in an oval of open sky; it is uncandled but alight, whitened by glare. I glance down the road ahead of me, then back up and locate again the patient, blood-hungry, peculiar chandelier in the pallid air. On its stringed circuit, on its heaven-descended chain, it marks in its circles the inclination of the lurching earth. I look down again and locate potholes and I steer some on the descending road and its shadows, and then I look back up again and to the side, and I locate the hawk but with more difficulty: it has shifted eastward. I try but I can't make out its markings; it is mostly a white blur plus a spikily black line swaying: the feathered edge of an airy paddle, mostly motionless on its own; but it moves anyway. The hawk. I hardly know how to look at it: man oh man oh man: the black, splayed-back pinions of the wings are like a fat boy's fingers gripping a windowsill of air. His head is hidden in blur; I am moving and can't see anyway—the pressure of wind is on my eyes. The road has its magical tunnel *descent.* When I look up again, the hawk is entirely gone, the sky is empty, the hawk's swing and my movements have covered more territory than time permits to be inside a single moment. So, it is another moment and a new territory. And there are more blocks to what I can see than I had thought to associate with the sky here, roofs, roadside cliffettes, and trees taller on this slope than on the other one, on the ascent. So, the sky is not wide here, it is not a great field in many dimensions but is a bunch of falling and rising glades or clearings of depth-y, height-y air, leaf-trimmed and almost exploding and zooming screens, here and there above me, through the failures of the trees along here to be fat and wild.

This slope of the ridge is more wooded and stylish than the ascent. The houses have more expensive yards among the trees; it is really mostly a woods here.

Again and again, my sight, diving upward, is a quick ballooning rush into blue particles, into stuff that has no resemblances but only a dissolving beauty—the planelessness—and the illuminated blue aerial substance of the day. My eyes are then lowered and fixed again on the striped and confettied road, and I squint ably in the wind and the downward rush.

And then a sexual rush buzzes along my ribs, and then a memory of white light, breathlessness: a flick, a flicker, which is a pinpoint of the vaster drowning, the convulsion of coming when I masturbate.

It's gone, and I have an erection that hurts. I'm me, a bicyclist, and there is Jimmy—I have a maybe brutal sense of romance.

"James—"

"Hunh—"

"God is The Great Pornographer."

He sort of says *hunh* again, noncommittally, not disapproving, maybe encouragingly. The wind pulls at the inflection.

I cannot bear the moment. Sometimes I think I know how Lucifer felt on the first morning when he saw creation and was overcome with feeling and resistance—and he fell.

"Does The Great Pornographer in the Sky, does he send you your sexual fantasies in color or in black and white?"

Jimmy listens to the blasphemy with caution: "Hunh . . ." This *hunh* is a signal that he's thinking. He slows down, marginally.

I hate him.

I catch up to him and blow and pursily push the syllables of a similar speech, a second reading.

"I don't know," he says. "I never thought about it."

He's afraid of the dark elevation of the mood, the subject—us being both in a kind of Secret and Happy Hell all of a sudden.

"Well, think now—" I know that sounds like a command, but the way I said it I was sad and not like a tyrant at all but just a guy who needed cheering up, sort of—this was partly a joke, partly a technique we all used, a lot of us, when we wanted to talk about sex.

The words, the subject spoonily stirs him. Jimmy gives in somewhat.

The wind blows his hair, my hair.

Twisted on his bicycle seat, he says, "They have a little color—sometimes."

"But when?"

He shrugged—*shyly.*

I offered, "Mine have color when they start, then they turn black and white." I spread out the idea, the sense of time in the idea, for him.

"Yeah, me too," he said shyly, and my heart started to beat with nutty interest, intimacy almost: we are at a more lightless vestibule of affection.

I am exaggerating the clarity with which we spoke, but things were clearer on this subject. We were more attentive even if we were also averted-ish, and nervous, in a lot of ways.

The words, simple monosyllables, were easy to hear, not much risk or effort in guessing at surface meanings anyway.

I said, "When I remember something sexual—it has real

color, like in real life, but I don't notice colors all that much.
I miss them if they're not there, but I don't keep track," I say.

"I think about colors a lot."

"You do?"

"Yeah."

"Oh."

We smile at each other in the quick slish-slosh of time, of
movements, of slight wind, the morning's air.

"If I try to imagine myself bicycling—if I make a fantasy—I
feel nuts if I notice things, because, for instance, the bike I use
in a fantasy may not be this bike—it can be on your bike—I can
be in midair until I think about which bike am I on? Then,
when I get the bike fixed up—when I notice and correct the
bike stuff—" Often, when I get a sentence halfway clear, I'll
suddenly play or romp into bigger words and more luscious
grammar "—then the memory starts to hurt, you know what
I mean, like a dream ache?"

I am showing off to him. He often lets me show off. Maybe
even *usually.*

The road is open to full sunlight again.

I had two veins running down my right forearm and one
ran along the side of the wrist and once crossed over the back
of the wrist and then forked, and there is the back of my hand
on the bicycle handlebars, the terrible white skin, the fairly big
fingers, the chrome bar and its curvature. There is the wind on
the new skin. Now I feel my back like a piece of plywood in a
sheet, a big board, a piece you can barely get your arms
around—*hug me, you bastard.* The bicycle seat rubs my ass and
the hollows of my skinny thighs—my right leg in particular.

"Like a dream ache—be-heep-, be-heep—do you hear me?
This is sore-ass Silenowicz. Jesus Christ, I hope these are some
halfway *decent* woods we're going to—" Me to Jimmy, unable
to bear the sexual stuff, and gasping some, pedaling alongside
him on a wide, empty stretch of road. This is in front of the
momentarily abandoned holes and girders of a shopping center being built. Hills of dirt, upright steel beams, enormous

open stretches to be made into a blacktop inland sea, an ebony Mediterranean of a parking lot.

I pursued the matter now of *my* complaint—I like complaint—the boyishly strained kind. I am experimenting with it. I should say, for one reason and another, I don't talk *much* at home or at school: so I dump on Jimmy, I dump a lot of words and elaborate constructions: i.e., ideas: "This is a lot of work to go to just to march around in some crappy woods—" I was, in part, doing an imitation or a version of a valid kid, not a creep. *Valid:* rooted in nature, male, meaning being stronger than some other kids, being bossy and in the position of judging other kids.

Wind interrupts my syllables, and he muffles and lids, defensively, his eyes, which he might otherwise use in part for amateur lip reading in the wind. We pedal: he sniffs, he smiles; he smells my speech, he smiles at it as if licking it inwardly; I mean it is a limp, vague, antenna-ish, plus devourer's, smile. *Is he friendly, the speaker,* the antenna part of the smile asks waveringly; *are his motives favorable,* it asks. If he feels uncomfortable smiling like that, it would mean I had been abominable and he had caught on fast. His smile tests my half-heard, barely heard, guessed-at speech, the secrets of its tones, of the future, of what I intend to do, of what I intend by it, my speech, my face in the moment, the pile-up of phrases, the different tones, the abrasiveness that is in part a mock abrasiveness to hide whatever soprano and witless *sweetness* has survived in me.

When his smile vanishes, that doesn't mean he disapproves of how I spoke to him so much as that his hearing me is a serious matter at the moment, more serious than the other matters—i.e., he doesn't want to run away from this topic so much—so he is attempting to hear in stages, depending on how much it's bothersome to him to hear me now that we mentioned sex for the first time this morning.

We move along on our slender machines among the conditions of travel: the potholes, the crookedly and swoopingly, centrally humped road, macadam, and pebbled; we bounce

and sway in the air currents and rush of nerves when a brushing, racing, wind-loaded and wind-spilling, bristling, and
snuffling boar of an automobile goes by—Christ, the weird
hissing and, neurally, the staggering hesitation of its passing,
then its dusty and advantaged, motor-steadied, keeled dimin-
ishing into the glimmering and dusty glow of distance with its
amazing speed: distance is golden this time of day, in this part
of the country, this part of the world.

The sun, at moments when it is sunny, heats the air, which
then rises like the ghost of a huge dairywoman, gray and yellow and of another century, and in the immense fluster of her
clothes, sounds are lost.

I am testing him, in part. If he makes a real attempt to hear
now, it will mean he is in a state of affection, even infatuation.
This test is and isn't purposeful on my part. I want to talk to
him, I am used to being with him, I mean, since we started out;
I am young and flexible in my habits; it's something I've gotten
into over the years, doing this, testing people but a little dis-
honestly, as an act of intimacy of a kind, as I'm doing with
Jimmy: but I really want to see if he is A Good Person. He's
An All-right Person (in some ways) but he is not good. But I
am so far out of control, so overfitted with energies and blus-
tering restlessness at this hour—this vacationer's day in my
life—that I am almost as pleased by his not listening, by some
blindness in his friendship as by the other. I'm almost as
pleased as if it were a sign of goodness, his being wicked or
whatever. Anyway, the goodness probably is not there. And
while I really can't live (or love) without it, I can't want it to
happen now. I'm probably safe. He's leaning back and just
pedaling, which indicates his vanity and my unimportance. If
he felt a lot of affection, he might listen and feel still more
affection, and common sense might leave him, and he might
come to me and cuddle and nurture me, here on these backward and decaying slopes of childhood, and I know fucking
well I would never be able to bear that. **Q**

Going Home to Mother

When I tell you about my "mother," you'll just shit. Everyone in the world thinks she's such a holy fucking saint. She came to a little town near Acapulco—one of the many called San Opportune—and erased a small portion of the world's guilt. But no one asked me, What about your mother? The real one.

Grace took me to her home in Rome and became my "mother." Gave me my own apartment next door to hers and a governess who didn't call me her little wetback. Grace taught me English, bathed me in *pane e cioccolato* and herself in public glory. But she wouldn't let me touch her power source, her library, and I didn't, until I was twelve and old enough to lie. This sagging, disagreeable, jealous woman's library was surpassed in size only by her wardrobe. (Though not wholly unsympathetic: she clothed me as well as she did herself and let me be good looking. With money and travel she was generous. But for the steady formation and development of my mental faculties, she had mostly jealous plans. This was a frustration I remember feeling well before I was ten, before I could even conceive of the real knowledge in her library; but although I couldn't count the number of volumes, I fully felt their power. But I gave Grace more grief than she deserved.)

Grace had made art criticism the profession of stars— forget being an artist. Her book *Sucking Off Art* was a best-selling manifesto that established her preeminence before I was born. Her articles could and did make careers, or end them. Oh, the hate mail! Conflict of interest wasn't considered a flaw; she was hailed for honestly building up the careers of her lovers and wiping them out when another came along. A new form of art criticism. People said she only slept with the great ones, but let me tell you Henry Packshaw Henry, for instance, isn't half as great a painter as he is a pain in the ass.

In fact, none of her friends had the stamp of moral value—perhaps the truest test of an artist—and even as a youngster this nagged at me in the deep bowels of my intuition. I seemed to remember that my real mother had taught me better, and this may account in part for my persistent ambition to return to my real home.

One day I saw Grace do a strange thing. She carried one of her furs to the butcher. Odder still, the butcher gave her a leather satchel full of cash in exchange. It was the intricate leather satchel that held my interest at first.

Later she claimed the fur had been stolen. More cash from the insurance company.

My new governess was not a very scrupulous person either.

Tranquila had taken pictures of our more intimate moments to blackmail my "mother" with. Unfortunately, as I explained to her, "mother" gladly would have published the prints herself, in a frenzy of art criticism.

So we brought the butcher a fur on our own initiative and found him untouched or unconcerned by interfamily squabbles, neutrality being his accustomed position. Neither Tranquila nor I had enough imagination or experience to bargain effectively with him, but after all a fur is a fur.

I said goodby to Tranquila at Leonardo da Vinci airport on my fourteenth birthday. On my way across the Atlantic, I was so excited to be going home that I jerked off three times under my cotton blanket.

I had four heavy bags filled with presents for my real mother and the brothers and sisters I figured I had, clothes, magazines, condoms and other personal effects, a gold brooch I gave myself as a going away present, six hundred dollars in cash, and Tranquila's necklace as a reminder of that scarce emotion, sentiment.

Still ebullient, I got in a cab at Kennedy and ended up paying one hundred and eighty dollars on the meter to get to the Plaza—this was 1970, folks—plus I gave a fifty-dollar tip. So much for sangfroid and savoir faire. I walked into the lobby and ordered a suite.

"For how many?" the bellhop asked.

I spun around comically, looked over my shoulder, under my crotch, then said, "It looks like just you and me, babe."

"I'm sorry, young man, the hotel does not accept unaccompanied minors."

The world is a skin-deep place, and truly beautiful people are recognized and rewarded as such. By truly beautiful, I don't mean the 95 percent of the human race that has a cute nose or long legs, sexy eyes or hands or redeeming features, pleasant looking and occasionally the love of a life, people who make a big hit at parties. I mean the one-in-a-million real beauties, people about whom there is no room for such a subjective thing as taste. They have the world coming in a completely different direction than it comes to the rest. People want to give to them, and that is a formidable, animal, power. They learn to use that power without ever understanding that others don't have it. They learn to receive gifts and adulation, and how to let knowledge and business, money and haute couture (my current field), simply come to them.

There is an early time, however, when the power is there but the control is not, and the power can be used by anyone who comes into contact with it. So it was with me, a great-looking kid with all the world coming to him, maybe.

But this was nothing in the way, a hotel clerk. "I am Grace ——'s son," I said. I was always ready to use "Mom's" name, and it often got me what I wanted. Sometimes more.

I had an open-ended ticket, and I decided to see New York before going home. Perhaps taking these couple of extra days was a sign of ambivalence.

My first visit was downtown, to the Figaro café. Raoul, the owner, had been a painter and Grace's lover years ago, when we were last in New York. She bought him the café in exchange for his series of six cadmium red canvases, each covered completely by a thin layer of munster cheese so that none of the red showed through. Cadmium is, of course, an expensive color, but it was worth it if you *knew* it was there.

I said hello. Since I was going to Mexico this week, he hoped I would come by in case he happened to have a little something for me to bring over there.

I went to the department stores and bought myself a suit. I went to a bar. I went to a club downtown and a bouncer checked my ID. The Last of the Red Hot Hippies.

A blonde appeared and said I was with her. This was enough for the bouncer and okay with me. Candy ushered me to a table and introduced me to her friends. I was partly disappointed, of course, since they were men, but I was curious as any outsider about the underground. For one thing, it was dark down there.

Barry, very tall and acne-scarred, boasted strangely: rock groups, writers, painters; Andy Warhol had been a personal friend; did I know "Bill" de Kooning—I did?!? I told him my name.

"Candy! That was your last chance!" He slapped the side of the table so violently that all the drinks spilled and fell off.

"But isn't he cute enough?" she sobbed, frightened suddenly. "Didn't you say to bring in some cute kid?"

"We can't use him! He's Grace ——'s kid."

"Well . . . then couldn't we kidnap him?" She looked at me apologetically. "I mean if it's okay with him."

"Tom!" Barry shouted. The bouncer came over. "She's through. She doesn't come back."

"Barry!"

"And get rid of this kid too. He's a minor."

"Barry! Please!"

The bouncer reached for her arm but she quickly kneed him in the balls. He took the table down with him, joining our drinks, which were obviously at the avant-garde. Barry pulled a comb out of his pocket, which handled correctly could fire one small-calibre bullet.

"Okay, I can take a hint," she huffed. I went out after her, but she hadn't waited for me. That was the end of the peace movement in New York City.

I spent two more days paying my respects to western civilization. Then I had one hundred dollars left and decided to pay the hotel. I felt kind of bad knowing I wouldn't have any more dollars for Mexico. I wouldn't get to play great white missionary, I figured, and they were going to have to be happy to just have me.

The hotel bill caused me a fit of impotence and fury. I tore the sheets off the queen-size bed and rolled myself in them, crashing into the floor lamp and breaking one of the legs on the TV console.

I went back to the Figaro café and told Raoul about my troubles. He was happy as hell to bail me out and I didn't stop to ask him why. But he wasn't doing it for the simple joy of giving.

After I got my bags downtown, we had a little talk in the back of the café, which became my new temporary home.

"Stick around a few days," he said, "and you can do me a favor"—which, he didn't have to remind me, I owed him—"you can take a package with you."

"A package of? Illegal?"

"My friend, at your age, nothing you do is illegal. Remember that."

This did not exonerate me from moral culpability, but that nicety is not what gave me pause. Fear was.

I got up to go, planning no return. "Okay," I said.

"Good. Sit down. Keep your trap shut. From now on you do only exactly what I say and nothing more or less."

I was assigned to the dishes, ostensibly because of my debt from the Plaza and because the dishes were piling up something awful. Raoul also set this muscular pygmy on me, and I couldn't eat lunch outside the kitchen without his company. I slept on a cot upstairs and m.p. slept in the same room so I couldn't sneak down the fire escape.

What was there to do but escalate the conflict?

"What are you, queer or something?" I smart-assed to m.p. He slapped my face and punched me in the gut. It took me half an hour to get my breathing normal again and three hours before I felt like wising off again.

"I bet you can't flex your brains as good as your arms."

Another smack, another move to my gut, but my knee was on its way up Candy-style, and m.p. was down brains first. I finished him off with a soup ladle to the medulla.

I took my bags and hailed a cab. The Waldorf Astoria, thanks again to Grace.

I called Raoul the next morning, and he was very sweet. "Mike, I was worried for you. Where are you? Let me send someone to pick you up."

"No thanks. I just called to let you know I was still in town. I'll call back later, but in the meantime I've got something for you to work on. I'll want some money wired to an address in Mexico," I said, sounding the depths.

"No problem, just give me the where and the how much. It's as good as done."

"I trust you, Raoul."

"You should, Mike."

"I also believe in the Easter Bunny, Santa Claus, and the infallibility of the pope." I hung up.

I ordered breakfast and put away four eggs over-easy, six slices of toast, a pot of coffee, a glass of orange juice, and the three muffins in the basket. I would have ordered more but I was too embarrassed at my appetite.

I went to Central Park and watched people neck on the rocks. I repelled the advances of a queer, watched little kids move in and around the kiddie zoo. Move like they've got no worries, they're not thinking about this or that, or about what their arms are doing. They run *vroom* in a crooked trajectory in and out of balance at the same time, and then maybe collapse onto a pile of other collapsed kids. An unpremeditated and yet not completely spontaneous pile. Their lightness and laughter and the careless flailing of their arms moved me to think about myself, although I can't explain the connection as it happened in my head. But I thought that a lot can change in a person, that they can become conscious of themselves in a short space of time, lose their grace, and that a lot of good looks and promise can go down the tubes. Or that worse, the wrong kind of promise could be fulfilled; personally speaking, that I could become like "Mom" or Raoul, on top but scared of the ephemeral value of all that I have.

I found a Woolworth's on Madison Avenue and broke my last fifty for a ten-dollar knapsack. I went back to the hotel and called Raoul.

"What's next?" he asked.

"Next is I go alone, no nothing, no bull. Goodbye."

"Bye, Mike," he said.

It was that easy to say no, I thought. I packed everything I needed from the four valises into the one knapsack, put the knapsack into a Macy's shopping bag, and I was set to saunter out of the hotel like one more guest on a shopping spree. I hoped I was like a little kid, discovering how to fall and land and coil up.

I took another cab, to Kennedy, and it cost less than fifteen bucks, tip thrown in. Imagine my surprise at seeing m.p. at the check-in counter, surely on orders, and lusting for revenge.

The police seemed out of the question and m.p. hadn't seen me yet, so I wheeled back around and back to the taxi line. I ordered dinner to be sent up at the Waldorf.

Suddenly I was a poor young wetback with less than twenty bucks and an inflated self-image. And how thrilled my mama would be to see her son, broke and bearing ridiculous gifts that probably wouldn't fit or have any value. After eleven years, her son would be back no better than he was to begin with and maybe more useless. And what was I going back for? A few hours of fiesta? Wet hugs from mama and maybe a scowl or two from the others? Maybe a private, well-deserved speech from the head of the family on how could anyone be so stupid as to throw away the only opportunity to get out of San Opportune.

I called the desk and got the international operator. Three minutes later I was talking to my "mother" the famous Miss ——.

"I thought I'd never hear from you again you little bastard."

"I'm in real trouble, Mom."

"I can imagine. You don't know the half of it."

"I'm sorry about the fur."

"No kidding? Well don't worry about me Michael, you know I can take care of my interests. Tranquila, on the other hand, . . ."

"Grace, I need your help."

"You're on your own."

"I used your name to get a suite at the Waldorf."

There was low whistle and then silence. Finally, "You sure don't stint when it comes to your comfort. That's a good sign."

"I had to. I was broke."

"And you were going to bring home oodles and oodles of pesos?"

Hoping to elicit some motherly concern, I said, "Raoul is forcing me to deliver a package to Mexico."

"I told you being a wetback would get you in trouble. Good luck to you Michael."

The line was dead. I was too late for innocence, too early for power.

I called Raoul back. "You're the boss," I said.

"Remember, Mike, you can't shit a shitter." He agreed to pay my bill again.

I emptied my knapsack back into a single valise, so I would look more ordinary going through customs. After delivering the package and stopping in at San Opportune with my presents, I'd come back to New York and work regularly for Raoul. Maybe do something less lucrative and more legal after I turned of age.

I didn't indulge in any self-pity, sure that I'd learn to handle my beautiful self, and that I'd get my hands on some books like Grace's, and that things would eventually flow toward me. The way things ephemeral attract light. I knew I'd have the wrong friends for many years. I promised myself to pursue something other than revenge and notoriety.

Just as I was leaving the room the phone rang. It was Miss —— with a change of heart if I skipped the trip to Mexico and just came back to Italy. As I said earlier, Grace never deserved all the grief I gave her.

I told her to go to hell. **Q**

Indians

They did it. They knew they shouldn't have done it, but they did it anyway. Oh no, they had done it again, and their mother had told them not to. The boy and the girl were in the bathroom looking at the tiles. The boy had his teeth clenched and the girl was fiddling with her hands.

"I told you not to do it."

"You didn't tell me anything," the girl said.

The boy pushed the girl aside. He walked out of the bathroom and closed the door behind him. He walked into the kitchen.

The girl followed.

"What are you going to do now?" the girl asked.

"Get out of my face," the boy said.

The girl sat down at the table and looked up at the boy.

"Well?" the boy said.

"Well what?"

"Well well."

"Well well you smell."

"Well?"

The girl said, "What do you think she'll do when we tell?"

The boy lifted his shoulders. The boy said, "I don't care."

The girl asked the boy if he was scared.

"No, I'm not scared," the boy said. "Why should I be scared, you did it."

The girl stood up and yelled in the boy's face, "I didn't do anything!"

"You moved it."

"You told me to move it."

"I didn't tell you to move it."

"You did tell me to move it. You said, 'Move it all the way

over to the side like this.' " The girl pushed out her hands. "Then you said to hold it so it wouldn't spill."

"You didn't hold it, did you? You let go. You always let things go."

"I do not," the girl said. She kicked the boy's leg. The girl got up from the table, then sat down again. "She's going to whip us bad," the girl said. "She's going to whip us until we scream." The girl said to the boy, "You think she'll whip us until we scream?"

The boy didn't answer.

The girl got up and walked over to the kitchen counter and turned on the TV. She looked at the TV. Then she looked away from the TV. Then she felt her head. "My head is hot. I'm burning up," the girl said.

"It doesn't matter. She won't care. She won't care if you have a cold or a bad bellyache or even a hot head. She won't care."

"Even if I'm real sick?" the girl asked. "What if I'm real sick and can't catch my breath?"

"She won't care if you can't catch your breath or if you can't walk or you can't talk, she'll give it to you anyway."

The girl opened her mouth but didn't say anything. She looked at the boy a long time, just looked at him, her head dropped to one side.

"There's no use looking like that. Just face it, you did it, it's already done now," the boy said.

"I didn't do it, you did it!" the girl yelled. "I was just trying to help you out."

"All right, all right," the boy told the girl. Then the boy walked over to the kitchen window. He looked out the kitchen window. It was sunny out, very sunny. The boy had to shield his eyes from the sun's glare. The boy thought of his mother as he stood there. He thought of her face. He thought of her arms. He thought of her hands.

She used to whip them with her hands, but now that they were older she whipped them with a strap. She used a strap, she said, because it was made of smooth leather that would never crack. It was a good whipping strap, and the boy knew that. It caught the air and whipped across the back of your legs. It made red spots back there.

The boy went back over to the table where the girl was sitting. The girl had her hands folded, and she was crossing her legs over and over again.

The boy wanted to pull her legs, just pull them to hurt her for messing up everything. The boy grabbed the girl instead, and they went back into the bathroom to look at the tiles. The tiles were just as they had been.

"Move away," the boy told the girl. "Get back." He closed the door of the bathroom again.

The boy and the girl went back into the kitchen and sat down at the table.

"When she comes in and sees those tiles, you're going to get it," the boy said.

The girl said, "You're going to get it too. Remember, we both did it."

The boy said, "Then after you get it, she'll take off what she has on and put something else on like she always does. It won't even matter that you're dead."

The girl said, "Maybe we could stop her before she gets there. Maybe we could lock her in the closet as soon as she comes in."

"There's no lock on the door," the boy said.

The girl said, "We could put a chair up to it."

The boy said, "She'll move it."

The girl started to cry.

"Don't start that. Don't start, you hear?" the boy said.

The boy pushed the girl and the girl held her mouth shut. Then the girl said, "I'm going to cry, I can't hold it."

The boy just turned his head. He looked at the clock on the wall. The clock on the wall said it was time.

The boy jumped up and ran over to the kitchen window. He saw his mother coming up the walk. He saw her face. He saw her arms. He saw her hands. She walked with her hands in a tight fist.

"I'm going to run out and tell her what happened," the boy said. "Then the whole thing will be all over with." The boy wiped his face with his hands. Then he ran to the door. The girl ran after him. They stood at the door and listened. The boy and the girl could hear their mother walking. They could hear her walking up the walk.

Just as she got to the door, the boy looked at the girl and the girl looked at the boy and then they both ran. They ran into the bathroom and they locked themselves in. They looked around at the tiles, then they looked at each other, then they looked at the tiles again, then they looked away from the tiles, then they just stood there. The boy had his teeth clenched and the girl was fiddling with her hands. **Q**

What Follows in the Wake of Love

Discover a man up before dawn out in his backyard smoking a cigarette, hushing up his dogs, and digging a shallow grave, and you've found yourself a man in love. Wamul Owens, who used to run the ice house over on the Southside, punctured his wife with an ice pick and kept her in cold storage for three months before I found her powdered with lime and sawdust. I'm the sheriff. Wamul said he wanted Lucille around, but didn't want her looking at the Norris boys no more. Fact is, your professional criminal avoids murder as an impediment to crime. But a person driven by love is deprived of reason, and you got to feel sorry for him. The criminal infliction of pain is genuinely impersonal and usually unpreventable. With lovers, however, pain becomes a sadly personal and often gruesome thing. This here's a story about love.

Three of our colored boys found parts of Gonzalla Hazard out in the slash pines, out there behind the Farm Labor Supply Center. Only way they knew it was Gonzalla was this tattoo of a crown of thorns on his left arm. "This kind of murder ain't normal," they said. "Something devilish going on." Gonzalla's woman said to me, "Sheriff, what's Gonzalla's babies going to do now?"

I know Gonzalla's got these two uncles living with him for the season, new boys to the county, from up around Indian River somewhere. Only got nine fingers and three eyes between them. I make it my business to talk to them first, and I find out right off that Gonzalla was over in Pahokee last Friday night at the Shuffle-Inn. Shuffle-Inn's this juke joint famous for troubles. Holy Rollers from the South Bay Pentecostal always trying to pray it out of existence, even worked some kind of hoodoo on it one time. I said, "You all with Gonzalla, Uncles?" thinking to myself that maybe I'm looking at the perpetrators right here on this rickety front porch. "Sure we was," they told me, "only we be asleep behind the produce mart by midnight."

I sent my deputy, Elvis Redwine's boy, up to Pahokee to ask some questions. What Kyle finds out is that Gonzalla and this little baby doll drank three, maybe four, bottles of Jax together and then checked into the Flamingo Motel out round back by the old depot. Kyle spoke with the Reverend Mangrove, who testified that he saw them, both of them, Gonzalla and Jezebel, that's what he called the sister, strut into that motel all tricked out like hot little circus monkeys, he said. Saw three people leave.

Meanwhile, I get a call from Mr. Flager. Mr. Flager wonders if it might not be wise to lock the workers inside the Center until the crime is solved, or at least until his crop is in. We've been down this road before, Mr. Wardell Flager and I. Sure, I could lock them up. For their own protection, I could say. Could do it easy. Find plenty of old boys around here like nothing better than swaggering around in the dark with rifles and dogs, earning themselves some county money. But I won't do it cause I don't think it's right.

Course, if I don't find the boy that done this killing, or the woman at least, I'm afraid we're going to have us some trouble. You know what the uncles told me? Told me they heard the pickers over to Cedell's Barbecue talking about signing off in the morning and driving over to Clewiston to work the cane fields. I said, "Uncles, you keep this news to yourselves."

Just the idea of all these beans rotting in his fields makes Mr. Flager mad. He kind of thinks this county belongs to him, and if he hears talk of migrants moving off before the harvest ends, I'll probably have to deal with those nasty fools he calls field bosses again. Intimidation is against the law, I've told him. Might as well talk to a cypress knee, though, as talk to a rich man about freedoms. Mr. Flager, he'll pass his tongue along his upper teeth and suck on that ivory toothpick of his. He'll give me that look. And then you just know my ulcer's going to kick up again. Be drinking milk and cream till I spit. Course the wife sees me on milk and she starts. She frets and sulks and calls the preacher's wife and then the preacher himself shows up for dinner one Sunday. She'll end up crying like she does, heaving her shoulders on the bed, making things worse. She'll leave me a note at the breakfast table. It will say, "Henry, I don't care about no new Studebaker. What am I going to do if you're dying in the hospital?"

You either hate this swamp and you leave it, or you hate it and you stay. Some, like Mr. Flager, stay on to wrest whatever they can salvage from the imposition of their wills on the land and the people. Most others stay because they can't leave. Too poor, maybe, or too limited. That was Mam's word for folks around Belle Glade. Mam left. Got tired of bleaching mildew from the kitchen walls, tired of cotton dresses clinging to her damp skin, tired of waterbugs in the larder and moccasins in the outhouse. "To live here, you got to breathe water, is all," Daddy would joke with Mam when she complained. Remember now, there were no ceiling fans then, nothing to cool the steam of summer air, and no canals or drainage ditches, no farms even, and no dikes holding back the lake.

This one night we're all sitting on the porch. Mam's rocking, slapping at mosquitoes as loud as she can. Daddy's telling me a story about how the glades were all under the ocean until this Indian god rose it up so his people wouldn't drown. Mam stopped her rocking. "Didn't raise it high enough," she says. "Decent folks ought not to live like this, Lester, like amphibians—never clean, never even dry, never safe or rested, always having to move to keep ahead of the predators cause nothing that stops can survive out here. I swear," she said, "even the damn grass has teeth."

Whenever Mam mentioned saw grass, that was my cue to fetch her bottle of Dr. Rowland's System Builder and her jam jar—"because ladies do not slurp from teaspoons," was Mam's explanation. Daddy, he's quiet like he gets until Mam, having swallowed her medicine, says that the Devil himself can take this land. Daddy's in the dark across the porch. I can't see him but I know he's making tiny circles with his finger on his bald spot. Daddy says, "At least it's our land." That was his answer for everything.

What we owned, and this was before Daddy lost it to a bank in the Depression, was half an acre, and you wouldn't call it land exactly, just a piece of this one vast, trembling mat sliding south from Okeechobee to the Keys. Centuries of rotted vegetation being sucked into the black muck. I used to think it was alive—the earth, I mean, the way the Indians did—from the noises it made and the smells it leaked. Made me think it was jealous of anything rising above it. Least, that's what I thought as a child.

I figure I owe it to the wife—the Studebaker, I mean. Carlene ain't been real well since her only child died the way he did. Donald was hers from the marriage with the musician. Made it all through Korea without a scratch, Donald did, comes home, mopes and pouts about the house, falls in with a shiftless crowd, and winds up impaled by a forklift at the packing plant in Loxahatchee. Pinned to the wall like a butterfly. I met Carlene while investigating the homicide. Suddenly, she needed someone to care for, and I was just as happy to get out of my trailer and into something more comfortable. But anyway, because she's a Baptist or something, or maybe because her family's related to the Wallaces of Boynton Beach, if that means anything to you, or for some reason I can't fathom, Carlene absolutely refuses to ride in my cruiser. She says she feels common in it. I tell her we are common. Trashy, then, she says. So I thought I'd buy us a car for our fourth anniversary. Nothing new, naturally, but recent like that '52 Pontiac coupe out at Tommy Kincaid's World of Cars. That way we'd have more time with each other and I could get her out of that house awhile. Maybe someday take a proper vacation. I've been to Tallahassee myself, to a sheriff's convention, and I think Carlene would like it there, the air-conditioned movie houses, smartly dressed people in restaurant windows, and all the work that goes on so cleanly inside of buildings.

"You ought to be searching those cabins along the lake, Henry," Mr. Flager tells me. I'm standing at the foot of his front stairs leaning up on the balls of my boots. "Come and sit, Henry." Mr. Flager motions me to the smaller of two wicker chairs on the verandah. We sit. Mr. Flager's wife, Julia, lives in an iron lung on the second floor—polio. Mr. Flager keeps a young thing not so discretely secured at the DeLeon Hotel in town. He goes on, "Her name's Lavonda Rose."

"Who's that, Mr. Flager?"

"The Jezebel at the motel. In Pahokee. With Hazard." He proceeds to tell me that this Lavonda and her male cohort must have driven back to Belle Glade with Gonzalla, forced him down a farm road, and murdered him.

"Why do you suppose they chopped him to pieces, Mr. Flager?"

"Is that important, Henry? Now see here," he says to me, "I've done your investigating for you. Now it is up to you to bring these criminals swiftly to justice."

"Mr. Flager, if you don't mind my asking, how did you come by all this information?" I said but knew, of course, that money is more persuasive than justice.

"I want my workers back in the fields, Henry. I'm making it your job to see that they are on that truck in the morning."

Mr. Flager's man, Julius, appeared on the verandah with a silver tray on which he balanced two tumblers of bourbon and a small black revolver, the drinks for each of us, the pistol for Mr. Flager. We thanked him.

"Mr. Flager, you can't force colored people to do what they don't want to do, not any more you can't."

"You amuse me, Henry." Mr. Flager sipped his bourbon.

"Seems to me you want things the way they used to be

before the war." And now I sipped. "It ain't ever going to be like that again, Mr. Flager. I'm sorry for you and your kind, but it just ain't."

Mr. Flager drew the pistol from his lap and cocked the trigger. "Perhaps you're right, Henry." He aimed and fired at the green anole sunning itself on the banister. It disappeared in a burst of splinters. "In the past, I suppose, I would not even have bothered myself with the death of a nigger." He replaced the pistol on the silver tray, nodded to Julius and stood. "Give my best to your lovely wife, Henry."

Kyle and I found Lavonda and her boyfriend out at Blondin's Fish Camp having themselves a regular honeymoon. They were tucked away in Cabin 14, windows closed, shades drawn, door locked. In a clearing to the side of the cabin sat these three filthy children, two of them chewing dirt, the eldest, a girl about seven maybe, scratching the ears of a spindly old hound. All four were silent. Gonzalla's Chevrolet stood in the scattered shade of a pine. Kyle tugged the floral drapery off the front seat, and we saw where blood had blackened the fabric. I took another magnesia pill and nodded to Kyle. The dog whimpered and the children stood. Kyle fired a round into the lock on the cabin door.

Mam asked could I bring my geography book home from school. I did and after supper me and her would sit at the table with a lamp and search through the pictures. One night Mam decided that Tennessee must be the roof of the country the way on page 95 the snow lay so thick and comforting in the Smokies. She told me there were reindeer in Tennessee, reindeer and penguins, even though that fact was not mentioned in the book. That comes in high school geography, she assured me. Reindeer, penguins, and log cabins with all their cracks chinked up with moss. Log cabins with fireplaces and electricity and indoor toilets. Mam said her sister, Elizabeth, the private secretary, lived in Gatlinburg and that we, meaning Mam and me, had been invited to visit her as soon as school let out.

Daddy said it's good you're going to see your sister and all, but the boy stays. I need him here.

For a while there were postcards, which I read to Daddy. Color vistas of mountains and fog and pastel-leafed trees. And then pictures of unusual buildings—a dairy bar shaped like a milkcan, a souvenir shop that looked like a teakettle, restaurants like tugboats, derbies and barrels of root beer. Mam sent one card of just a blue Greyhound coach. A forward window was circled and arrowed. MY SEAT she had printed. Daddy said, "She don't own it."

Then Mam wrote that some clever Yankee doctors had advised her not to return so quickly to the thick, damp, tubercular Florida air. Since she no longer wished to burden dear Elizabeth, she would travel instead to Chicago. She only hoped her lungs were not already beyond salvation. The next spring Mam wrote that she had landed a job at a boarding house frequented by commercial travelers. That's when Daddy told me. Took me, in fact, to the O-kee-doke Club, bought me my first beer, and me only eleven or twelve, and says, "Son, your mother never had no sister."

Now Carlene's case is like the opposite of Mam's. When her Donald was only six months old, Carlene's husband, a cornet player, went off to do a gig in West Palm and never came back. Never wired money. Nothing. What Carlene should have done is called those Wallaces in Boynton Beach to come and fetch her and her child. But she is a proud woman and would not allow herself to be seen in the harsh light of poverty and abandonment. And she could not write to her father, a circuit rider in south Georgia who had disowned her following her elopement. Preachers are often quick to disinherit and sluggish to forgive. Still, she had the house, and she stayed and raised her boy with the eventual help of her second husband, a junior-high football coach whose last wish as he lay dying of emphysema was that Donald join the army and defend his country.

. . .

So the two of them's lying on the floor oblivious in the middle of the one dark room. She's on her stomach, face covered by the damp blanket of her hair, wearing one of those Japanese kimono deals all the soldiers brought back from the war. Large scarlet-and-lemony flowers on her shoulders like she'd fallen into a garden. The man's on his back snoring, sweating and shirtless, with one leg draped across her butt, and when Kyle kicks him conscious, he's staring down the barrel of Kyle's shotgun. Across the room, the green dial of a radio glows and Hank Williams is singing a song about someone not loving someone like they used to, which is funny, you see, on account of Lavonda herself is null and void on narcotics and the boyfriend turns out to be a deaf mute Seminole name of Andrew Jackson, so Hank's just pleading into the void until me and Kyle come along.

Andrew Jackson's from Big Cypress we find out, and until last Friday wrestled alligators at a snake farm on 441 across in Hendry County. Seems Friday, Andrew was fired for killing a thirty-five-year-old fourteen-foot bull named Rex who'd been all along the farm's star attraction. Like falling from a bar stool after that, I imagine. Falling all the way to this musty cabin on Okeechobee, passed out on a linoleum floor with a wilted hooker and her, or someone's, three children, and wanted for murder. Andrew Jackson began sobbing and shook Lavonda's shoulder. Kyle said, "I wonder what she's dreaming about." Probably love, is what I thought. Kyle tapped his foot to the music and I had this crazy notion right then that this rendezvous here was in a way romantic—out here by the lake, away from the world, yourself and a woman, the radio's on, the drinks are like fire, you talk and love until you find some peace. With a car, I thought, Carlene and I could drive ourselves to some secluded bungalow just like this. I said, "Kyle, shut down that radio."

"She be spawning now, Sheriff," the uncles tell me. Gonzalla's woman, writhing like an eel on a skillet, is giving birth to the last of Gonzalla's children on the floor of this tenant shack. I've come to tell her something about the murder. Uncles tell me I got to be the doctor. "Doctor catches the baby, that's what," they say. I kneel between the great brown thighs and immediately a smooth, leathery child slithers into my hands. I want to wipe the foam and blood from its face, but he's squeezing my wrist with his tiny hands, each with four padded digits. "That's for sure one of ours," uncles say. "Just look at those webbed toes." I study this arrowheaded, horny-lipped thing and notice the feathery pink gills below the ear-holes. They must lose those when they're weaned. I wanted to see did it have a tail, but that's when the dream ended and I rolled out of bed so as not to wake Carlene, and dressed to meet Mr. Flager's truck at the Center.

The field hands, some more hungover than usual, met the truck at dawn, and so did Mr. Flager, pleased to see that his harvest would now be completed in an orderly fashion. He congratulated me in front of the workers for solving the murder so swiftly, which only he and I and his informer knew was not at all true. It was at once a magnanimous gesture, which I truly appreciated, and a calculated charade that I just as deeply distrusted. Meanwhile, Gonzalla's woman had found herself a new man and told me that the children weren't none of Gonzalla's nohow. He was just another mouth to feed, is all, she says. Sounded like the words of a woman scorned and still fatally in love. Her new man, a yellow-black from up north named Roosevelt Holmes, sent the uncles packing. Said them few gnarly fingers gave him the willies.

By the time the trial commenced, Gonzalla's little family, along with this Roosevelt and just about anyone else who might have had an interest in the fate of Gonzalla's killers, had vanished from Belle Glade—the workers to follow the harvest north to the Carolinas, Mr. Flager to do whatever it is he does in Havana with his sweet young thing, and Gonzalla's accumulated remains to his mama up in Forest City, Arkansas. The zealous Reverend Mangrove, however, became a fixture at our jail. He had appointed himself Lavonda's spiritual advisor. Every afternoon at one he came wearing his iridescent green suit and porkpie hat and wiping his brow with a white handkerchief.

Lavonda confessed and threw herself on the mercy of the court. Confessed that she and Gonzalla had been carrying on an intermittent harvest-time love affair for seven years and that one or possibly two of her children belonged to Gonzalla. Confessed that Andrew Jackson was a sexual powerhouse whose carnal nature drove her to a frenzy. Confessed the grisly details of the night in question. What began, according to the prosecuting attorney, as a relatively innocent sexual diversion, in which Gonzalla was bound and gagged and forced to watch Lavonda cavort with Andrew Jackson, escalated into something bestial, unthinkable, and yes, gentlemen of the jury, fatal.

Lavonda confessed that Andrew Jackson just sort of snapped the night they did Gonzalla, probably because he lost his job, she figured, or maybe, like the reverend says, he was into some kind of Satan worship like so many of those pagan Indians are. Something had made him furious, she just couldn't be certain what. He suddenly went at the little man, slicing him with a fish knife, and began to fillet him like a bullhead, while all the time Gonzalla's screaming for mercy and whatnot cause he's still alive, you see. She knew it was wrong, what they done, but at the time, Judge, she said, at the time, to be quite honest—having placed her left hand on the Bible and sworn before her personal Lord and Savior, Jesus Christ, to tell the whole truth and nothing but—to be truthful, she was kind of excited by it all, by her strapping Seminole lover, the starry night, the Chevrolet, the money in Gonzalla's billfold, all these sudden changes in her life. Of course, now she was sincerely sorry that it all had to happen. You can see for yourself she's telling the truth, her lawyer says. Lavonda was found guilty of prostitution, aiding and abetting a felon, etc., and given a three-year suspended sentence so that she could see to her children, and ordered by Judge Lanny Purvis to attend weekly pastoral counseling sessions at Reverend Mangrove's Rose of Sharon Free Will Baptist Church.

Andrew Jackson was not so fortunate. Of course, he did not testify, since he could not, but he did affix his mark and his thumbprint to a confession drawn up by his own attorney. And he did act out his own slow-motion version of the murder right there in the courtroom with Kyle playing the part of Gonzalla. Andrew might see his next alligator around 1986, if there are any left by then. More than likely, however, he'll wither and die in prison inside a year. They always do, those Indians.

I took Carlene out for a test drive to make sure she liked the way the Studebaker handled before I put my money down. Tommy says, "You all take whatever time you need to get to know this beauty, Sheriff." We headed out 98 along the canal to Twenty-mile Bend. Carlene got hold of her kerchief under the chin and she stared straight ahead and every once in a while she said, "Slow down, Henry, please. My hair."

At Twenty-mile, I pulled to the shoulder and switched off the ignition. Carlene sat silently. I heard the ping and tick of the cooling engine. I examined the dashboard and gripped the steering wheel. We watched a gray carpet of field rats ascend from a drainage ditch and swarm across the highway onto a cornfield. Away across the field, we saw a sharecropper and his children hoeing along a row.

"Well, what do you think, Carlene?"

She looked at the hands folded in her lap. I looked at them. I almost touched them.

"Happy anniversary, Sugar," I said.

"I don't want it," she said.

"But, Honey," I said, "this ain't trash, this is a Studebaker."

"I'd rather have a Maytag," she said.

"But you can't ride in a Maytag," I said.

She said, "Wherever would we go, Henry? It's just swamp and more swamp."

I mentioned maybe Boynton Beach or Tallahassee. Said we might could spend our anniversary weekend in one of those hideaways along the lake.

"Don't!" she said. Carlene gripped the hem of her dress with both hands. "Take me home now, Henry."

At the house I told Carlene to go ahead and order the washer from Sears and Roebuck, gave her a peck on the cheek, and said I was going for a ride. I drove for Pahokee.

All this complaining about the cruiser, then, had been Carlene's way of telling me—without having to say it—that she didn't want to go driving at all. Only she didn't want to hurt my feelings, didn't want to admit that staying in that house is more important than stepping out with me. I should have seen that, should have read between the lines, guessed that her way of leaving the swamp is to hide in the house she shared with the two husbands and the child who'd left her.

I've known this about Carlene from the first—that all she ever does is care for people. It's almost her job, how she finds meaning in life. If I were gone, say, she'd have to find someone else to take care of, or she'd die. But she's afraid to have a person care for her except in that vague, Christian way like they do at church. Given her matrimonial history, you can understand her caution, maybe. If someone cares for you and then leaves, that's naturally worse than a stranger leaving, isn't it? But on the other hand, when folks leave, they can't hurt you anymore and that in turn makes them easier to love, I guess. But what I've gone and done is force Carlene to acknowledge something she did not want to. I wish I hadn't. As I drove, I thought about her back home looking through her photo album again. She'll wind up all sweet and quiet, out on the back porch, rocking dreamily, and staring into the chinaberry tree.

In Pahokee, I parked across from the Flamingo on Lake Street. Looks like a lot of motels built after the war—L shaped, yellow brick, flat roof, red doors with black numbers. Gonzalla's final room was Room 6. Out on the street a fifteen-foot formerly neon flamingo stands in a plot of weedy earth bordered by boulders painted white. To see it now, shabby like it is, broken rain gutters, littered lot and such, you wouldn't recognize it as the symbol of optimism it was in 1946 when land speculators and developers tripped over each other trying to buy up any moderately dry plot they could find hereabouts. Take a look at the postcards on the registration desk and you'll see how immaculate and confident it looked then.

I sat in that car watching and waiting for answers. I watched for maybe ten minutes. I saw a cloud of sulphur-colored moths rise up from the castor-bean plant growing against the side of the office. I saw Mr. Patel, the Pakistani owner, walk toward Room 4 with a stepladder and a garden hose. I saw him kick open the door and go in. You're a sheriff long enough, you begin to notice details like the Dodge pickup with the Virginia tags parked at the office door. Details that might unexpectedly turn into trouble or suddenly help you solve a mystery. I noticed a blue vinyl and chrome chair outside Room 12, the heat shimmering off the roof and off the cracked asphalt of the parking lot, a child's red tricycle on its side at the top of the trash bin. Gonzalla, what drove you from your family's arms to this motel again and again?

You're a sheriff long enough, you realize that every criminal has a motive, every man has his reasons. You don't know what it means to want so intensely that you let your children eat dirt while you make time with your old man. You can't figure that kind of desperation, maybe, but you know there is some terrible logic at work, the kind that frees a person to do what he is impelled to do.

. . .

At the Flying A, I check the oil and the radiator, fill it with ethyl, and drive north, not to anywhere really, just north away from the heat and the silence and the inevitable dampness. Vanished is what they'll say. Been under a lot of pressure or something. Someone will remember Daddy and how he blew out his brains in the lobby of Mr. Flager's Belle Glade Five Cent Savings Bank, and they'll shake their heads. Drive for two days clear to Gatlinburg. See the Atomic Diner shaped like a big mushroom cloud, but that's as close as I get to Mam. She never thought I'd come looking for her. That's how crazy she was. So crazy she up and left her husband and child and started a new life simply because the old one was intolerable. Drive so far north I see snow for the first time and sight my first penguin. Of course, I don't do any of this. I stare at the Flamingo. Then at the backs of my hands. Then back at the motel. I'm not crazy like Mam was or Daddy even. I'm steady. No one will ever have to remember me because I'll be here.

There's a pot of black bean soup simmering on the stove and a note scotch-taped to my bowl. TAKE YOUR MEDICATION, it says. BEER'S IN THE ICEBOX. I'VE GONE TO BED WITH A HEADACHE. LOVE, CARLENE. I put her note in the cookie jar with the others. We've been together these four years and we still don't talk much. I thought it would get easier. Instead, she's learned to write notes, considerate and tender notes, and to get migraines. I've learned to stay at work and let this ulcer burn a hole in my stomach. It's the best we can manage, but it's all right. I mean that. We have come to depend on each other to be cautious and deliberate and distant. We know we are living on perilous ground that might sink as surely as it rose.

I turn off the burner under the soup, undress in the bathroom, and tiptoe to bed. Carlene has her back to me. I know her eyes are open, but I don't let on. I clear my throat, give her a chance to toss, turn, pretend she has woken. And what would I say if she did? I'd say Carlene, a person would know if his mother were dead, wouldn't he? Mam would be seventy something now. I picture her sometimes rocking by a fire with the radio tuned to a soap opera. But I don't like to think about that. I close my eyes—I'm eleven or twelve and I'm with my mother and our whole lives are ahead of us. We're on a snowy mountain in Tennessee on the roof of the country; Mam's holding me to keep me from falling. **Q**

George Isn't It

"Where's Dottie? What have you done with my Dottie?" She's dangling the pink plucked chicken, dancing it by the wings in her hands over the new white double sink she finally got to order from Sears last year and that the hired man put in with a wrench and with his knobby can-do-anything hands, those tough-as-shoes-and-all-over-everything-and-not-caring-if-they're-dirty hands of his. The sink and the chicken and her face all glisten wet and shine in the light from the window where dozens of flies are circling and diving for our side of the screen.

She's got her big, blue-dress back to me, but she turns and peers through her skin-colored glasses over her big blue shoulder at little-kid me standing by the screen door, and she's looking right at me, and I'm saying, "It's me! I'm Dottie!" and I'm stamping my foot on the linoleum and I'm thinking she must be playing with me, but she's looking right at me and the chicken's still dancing headless in the sink and the flies are still diving into the screen and her soft, old face with the pink plastic glasses looks like no kidding.

"Oh no you're not," she's saying, and she turns her big and blue back around, "You must be somebody else—you must be somebody I don't know. My Dottie would never stamp her foot and talk back to me the way you're doing! I don't know who you are!"

I'm standing wordless looking at her blue back wiggle back and forth as she's cutting the chicken over there across the shiny black-and-white flecked green linoleum. She's talking, "You go and tell the real Dottie that whenever she's ready to come back in here and start acting like her own self then I'll talk to her and no one else until then!"

The real Dottie? The real Dottie? I look down at my legs and feet and sandals and they're the same. Maybe this means I won't get any fried chicken tonight, but I'm not going to cry—I'm not going to let her see me cry—I'm pushing on the scuffed screen door that always sticks and that also came from Sears, but a long time ago, and that the hired man was supposed to fix but the weather keeps changing on it and then it's unfixed again, and I push and it bangs open and then shut, and she's saying, "And don't bang that screen door on the way out!" as I'm going down the back steps, of which there are seven, and I hop down them one by one saying, "Dottie, Dottie, the real Dottie, I don't care, I don't care, I don't care."

Flies are buzzing all over the scrawny wild kittens I already chased all morning, and they are all lying limp under the porch where it's not so hot. Even then they're not so easy to catch as I first thought they'd be, seeing them crazy-wild in the barn when I first got out here, and right then I spotted that one yellow one I've gotten to where he'll almost come to me, and when he does come to me I'm going to do what the hired man said and cover him all over with bacon grease, which he will hate and will run from in circles all over the farm, and the other wild kittens will wonder what is wrong with him since they won't have to have it on them, but the thing is that it will smother all his fleas and then he will lick it off and then he can come sleep on my bed in my room and have a name and be mine. And those other kittens will grow to rove the country-side, skinny-wild and youthless, diseased and hit by trucks, belonging to no one. Even when we see them they will not be seen, like rats and squirrels, for any one of them seems like all the others—giving birth and dying young and never having names. When I go near they all run back up under the house, even that yellow one that I have chosen to be the one that's going to be mine, looking out at me with their little eyes. The one that's going to be mine has one blue eye and one green, both eyes looking out like they've never seen me before. "I'm

Dottie," I say to him lowlike and hold out my hand past the zinnias and make noises, but he doesn't know me.

I will go and find the hired man, and he will know me, and he will talk to me and let me follow him around while he works, usually at this time of day on the other side of the chicken yard, but I don't see him out there now.

There's a horned toad! A horned toad scoots and stops and scoots across the yard and out toward the barn! I'm running after it across the patchy grass and I'm climbing the fence and climbing the fence, and jumping down from the fence, and now I don't see him! Where did he go—out to the barn maybe. I've lost the horned toad. Maybe it's the same one I was playing with yesterday out here—stroking his white, smooth, horned toad's curving belly until he was unable to move, just like I do to the other horned toad named Lucy that's mine and that I keep in a box back at the house. If I could be sure he was the same horned toad then I could call him Max and bring him food, but maybe he would rather run free and do without.

The hired man's out in the barn—I'm pretty sure of it. I know he is because I don't see him around anywhere for one thing. I like to go out there or wherever he is working because he likes to talk about all the things he knows, which is all about everything, it seems to me—all the names of things and how to do things—and I like to watch his round shiny arms lift things and his big hands, rough as the toads on the back with undersides tough and silky smooth, which are wise with animals and even with things like the tractor.

The milk cow and the mama cat are sleeping out here in the barnyard, both flicking flies with ears and tails, heads resting on the pounded-down-to-powder-smooth black dirt with its jagged cracks like broken cake and, once in a while, a tuft of weedy grass. It's too hot to move, but it seems to me they know I'm here, that they have seen me before and they know who I am. I take a stick and write in the dirt, D O T T I E, then rub it out with my foot.

The big dark cool barn is damp with smells like rolling on the lawn—smells that make your mouth water. Mud daubers and yellow jackets fly the tall openings—their bodies flash in the sun, flash-vanish into high dark rafters out of sight.

Back in the back a room sits with the hired man in it. Sometimes he sleeps back there in the back on a cot, no clothes on and brown all over. Because I've seen him is how I know. I'll go get him to tell me about things. It's not so dark in here now that I can't see the door back there, which is almost, but not quite, closed—it's not so dark as all that. Bright white squeezes through cracks and corners and lights up long ribbons of dust that stand in the air. Near the door I see brown feet on the cot, but mustn't creak the door, and I listen, sandals off and the cool dirt a drink of water to my hot white feet, I hold my breath and the hired man breathes a long deep intake all the way down and then long it comes out again, back out and out again, and a faint voice under as if the wind was coming up outside. The hired man is asleep.

Stomach in, slipping through the crack in the door, I'm listening for breathing and holding my own, and there he is, big body stretched on the cot, a little toward the wall and asleep, clothes all heaped on the floor with stacks of magazines and Sears catalogs. A light bulb dangles above the cot and some flies zoom back and forth across the room banging into the walls. And he's breathing in and out with his hired-man's heart so big and strong that I can see his body and the cot and, it seems like, the whole room shaking to its rhythm.

If only I knew the hired man's real name—because I've heard it said that George isn't it—I would call him by it right now, but instead I whisper what we all call him—George—thinking if he's awake he will hear that, but he doesn't move, and maybe like the wild kittens the hired man doesn't have a real name at all, like if a person could be born and die without a real name—but if George were to die we would probably then find out what his real name was, and then I would be able to touch him without him knowing I was doing it—if he were to die, I mean.

But the hired man is asleep and breathing like I am breathing, and his heart is beating like my heart is beating, and now I am standing so close that I just reach out and touch his back with one hand very lightly, and at that same time I am saying lowlike, but out loud, "I am Dottie, aren't I, George? Who else could I be if I'm not Dottie? George, George, wake up and tell me I am Dottie!" And then he kind of jumps, like if I scared him, and as I step back the hired man rolls onto his back and I see that that thing he's got that boys and men have and that if you're a girl like me you hardly ever get to see one—that thing is big and pinkish and sticking up in the air, sort of dancing around shiny like I've never seen before—and right at that moment a big horsefly lands right on the pink tip-end of that thing, and then George sits straight up kind of like asleep but his eyes wide open and looking right at me, and he shouts out, "Linda Sue! Linda Sue! Is that you, Linda Sue?" **Q**

Listening to Jesus

During the long, do-nothing summers, when my out-of-the-coal-mine-into-the-wine-barrel uncle, as my aunt would always call him, would tell my aunt and Jesus-to-Christ-listening that he was anymore all-too-alone-crazy watching the grapes turn black all day on the farm, with the Mexicans looking at him like he was a scarecrow on the property and not any kind of man who belonged to the property, tending to good purpose on it, but just stuck there to draw yellow jackets and to trap gophers all day long and play Gin Rummy to nobody else in the kitchen all night only, because he had not two lousy cents and a dime to go the half mile down the road to the Injun Hut to get himself even a draw of what piss water they got off the tap, my uncle said, like any other white man walking on the surface of the earth with something to do partnered up to other hands human, and not to just the goddamn gopher he was going to catch, by Christ Heavenly, who was even starting to look down his nose at him, my all-too-alone-crazy uncle would say, down his nose and then only going back in at the last minute anymore, as if even the gopher knew what even a scarecrow looked like, and that leaving him out there to be dogged to by a dumb dog in front of every passing picker was not the right way, by Christ Jesus, to treat a man who was of the same blood as my aunt and my father, running there in any blue vein he could point to on his still-good-for-something arms, besides just to be a stick-stuck empty shirt in the wind without not the two cents and a dime in his pocket to sit among men for half an hour before going back to a house black with night, without not even sound inside of it except the dog nails on the linoleum and a short leg of log burning up in the stove just for the sound of it burning or to heat up some all-week-old Mulligan stew that he could not anymore look at by himself, my all-too-alone-crazy uncle would say—during the long of those summers when there was a farm still for us to go to, my out-of-the-coal-mine-into-the-wine-barrel uncle would sometimes stumble up the driveway back in the city, a day or two days stray before the sometime Saturday when we would all go out to the farm together—stumble up to the back porch door with his hands in his pockets, saying right to me or to my aunt, who would always come down from upstairs, or to one of my sisters, or just to the things he would look at hard, that he was no good to Jesus anymore for it, not at night like that anymore out there alone, without not two cents and a dime to jiggle in his pocket in a place where more than just his two feet and a dog's stood together—no good to man-my-God-to-Jesus anymore for it, and that he would rather tap out a few mayonnaise jars or pickle jugs of red to a passing Mexican so he could give the money to the bus driver and ride the bus in, like a man with a still-good-for-a-pick-and-shovel couple of arms and legs on him—ride in and not have to walk the sixty-odd like a beggar to see his blood-own, face to face around a table, before the sometimes all-together-skipped-over-forgotten odd Saturday when nobody would care to remember, my all-too-alone-crazy uncle would say, remember that he was even out there like a shirt stuck on a haystack, with a dumb dog to feed, always breaking the chain every week whenever a yellow jacket got under his tail, and that he would rather tap the red in his veins all day and all night for just the bus money, before he would ever leave that black house to tramp down to the Injun Hut at night with whatever vat-soaked money he could get and let a rag-on-a-scarecrow pickled-up Mexican buy him a wrist-jerk or a long-arm of what piss-water they got pissed out that night for the "peace-to-what-ails-you."

Then my aunt would ask my all-too-alone-crazy uncle if he had fed the dog, if he had remembered to open a can for the dog, and my uncle would never be able to remember who ate the week-old rest of the Mulligan, he or the dog, or if he had paint-stick-poked-out a half can for the dog or not out into the cast-iron fry pan by the dog house where the yellow jackets were, or if even he had remembered to lock up the back porch door to the house out there for certain, and my aunt would say to my out-of-the-coal-mine uncle that he had his head in the barrel again, that he was a man walking around with his head in a barrel that my father or my other uncle—her good husband, next-as-close-to-blood-own—would bust open with a hammer from the garage if they caught sight of him come in no account stray to home, leaving the sheep to the wolf, just to wet his cork local to home and neighbor, leaving a dumb dog tied up to die on the line and wine smell all sweated out wet under his armpits to a stink still all over on him for just anyone to smell besides only herself, my aunt would say, and that he had but short of one-half hour to eat a salami and cheese sandwich sit-down, before he had to get right back up on that bus and go back, like the Good Shepherd who would not ever desert us, and that he could have me to take along for the company, if that would put the cork on him, to play his goddamn-always Gin Rummy with, if that was the ticket, and to take twenty dollars to pocket—her run-out nylon own money—to get at least a bag of flapjack flour and canned milk and some kibble for the dog if it was not yet dead, and an Eskimo Pie for me, the boy, to hold things over until they, the rest, got there to put the tin lid back on things, the next tomorrow or the tomorrow after that, depending on what day stray it was that time, and my aunt would tell my out-of-the-coal-mine uncle then to take his wine-soaked shirt off for her to wash with all the rest, and to put on a clean, same-size work shirt of her husband's and a clean undershirt too, and to do it all in three specks less to the half hour, by her clock counting, and I would sit down then with my uncle and eat a baby skinned potato out of the blue roaster or a ladle of lentil soup or pink bean soup with blubber-thick pieces of home bacon in it to just leave in the bowl, or maybe just a fat piece of hard-to-get-the-scalp-off salami and the little kind of pickles that my aunt always put with it that took a little speck second to put on a plate, she said, and then my aunt would go to get me gum for my pocket out of her black purse in the bedroom drawer and I would take the box that had the big black ace of spades on it out from the scissors-and-string drawer in the kitchen and put it in my button-up sweater pocket, and my out-of-the-coal-mine uncle would say then, that I was a crook, that I had eyes in my head already crooked to crook him on the bus, and my aunt would tell my all-too-alone-crazy uncle to crank up his lip and drink down the water she put for him and get going to wait for the next bus coming before her good husband or my father came home and put wheels to his barrel and rode his wine-soaked head over every last bump in hell.

Before anyone could come to put wheels to his barrel, my uncle and I would take a paper bag of apples for the bus and run-walk down the cement driveway to the sidewalk, where I would go out past the yard-long redwood fence first to see if just maybe there was a Buick turning this way by the light or if my father was maybe turning that same two-blocks-to-walk big street corner, walking under the always pink-on neon-lighted sign that said COCKTAILS in neon-tubed writing under a skinny-up-to-the-V-topped glass with a supposed-to-be neon cherry sitting down in the V-bottom of it, and if there wasn't any Buick or just my father coming, so that we might have to go out the backyard good-neighbor gate and walk across the good-neighbor flagstone-set-in lawn and down the good neighbor's driveway to take that side street, my uncle and I would take then, the always best short-cut to the big store street, the long of those summers when my uncle was a day or two stray and all-too-alone-crazy come back to know exactly what day it was or what barrel he was supposed to be in, he would tell me, but just only knew where by Christ, the big bus stopped that was going our way, to the place where the fancy buses were too high-tone to go, my uncle said, and did not stop just in front of the Five and Dime anywhere like this one did, where he said he knew just the where it stopped, just the

nickel-and-dime good-for-nothing place where the big old
Peerless would clunk open a front wing door like a chicken
does its wing, I thought, and take even Jack-anybody in if he
could come up with the ante, my uncle would say, in right in
front of the nickel-and-dime here and dump him Jack-out-of-
the-barrel into piss-water nowhere, my out-of-the-coal-mine
uncle would tell me—us running-walking the short way to go,
through the gravely back of the donut shop parking lot, where
my father coming home or my other, next-as-close-as-blood-
own uncle, driving home in the Buick, were not so likely to
walk or drive through—us running-walking to catch the big
one different in the distance from the other yellow and green
all-the-time-running city buses, the ones that ran past the Hag-
strom's and the bakery and the toggery store where we always
got socks and handkerchiefs for my father, with the no-headed
suit-men stuck on pole-stands in the window—us waiting for
the speck of minutes left in front of the red-signed Five and
Dime for the big, cut-corner-front-windowed bus to come and
get us and stop for certain like my uncle said he knew it would
stop, and open out the door slow, to me and to my out-of-
the-coal-mine uncle—the different-opening, nothing-to-see-
through, big metal door that we would have to walk way out
away from the curb to stand out in front of closed up tight, and
then stand back away from for the door to make the cranking
sound starting, and then the metal wing pulled-back clunk
sound that the door made when the metal wing-bone lever
flat-locked to open, like the sound that my other uncle made
when he hammer and chisel-hunked the metal rings down
around the wine barrels to make them tight, I thought—me
clunking up the rubbered steps of the bus then, and my uncle
clunking up behind, reaching, as I waited, for the money that
my aunt had given to him to pocket, and pinching the one bill
that I could see was a twenty into a long, bent-over V-shape
to give to the bus driver, while the driver pulled in the stick-up
handle and the wing door closed back shut, and I would
chicken-walk toward the back first, crooked along the narrow

aisle, high with big brown seats with what I could see of people, here and there, sitting in them, and my uncle would stumble behind, holding onto the soft brown tops of seats by
people's heads sometimes, with a half-fistful of bills in one
hand and two skinny brown tickets stuffed into the half-fisted
other hand—me, crooked down to my shoes in the going bus,
crooked as a spare Jack, cut-corner-bent-in a little on the one-
eyed and on the two-eyed ones that I liked always to grab up
no matter what, whenever we played Gin Rummy or Jacks or
Better—me, crooked from my eyeballs down to my chicken-
split feet, my uncle would say, looking for a pair of empties so
I could climb up in and be by the window and see all as much
of the where-we-were-going-to before it would get to be dark,
when my uncle would turn on the baby bulb light under the
metal rack over our heads that sent a cone-shaped tower of
light, small to big, down to the itchy fuzz brown bus seats,
where my uncle would snap down his no-good-to-a-hill-of-
beans spades or sometimes turn over his good-enough-to-win
pair of kings—the light that was like a real beacon, I thought,
and not like the little soft spread of moonglow around the top
of the tiny plastic lighthouse plugged into the wall of the
bedroom that my aunt would turn on at night so that I could
go to sleep in the rest of the dark—and my uncle would say
that he didn't care who ever won the game so long as nobody
crooked him, so long as he knew the-when-to-get-off-the-
barrel and the crooked damn bus driver, crooked for taking a
damn straight three dollars for just a chicken-split kid, knew
anyway the goddamn-where-he-was-going-to, my out-of-the-
coal-mine uncle would say—knew the place the way my uncle
said he knew places in the world, the ones he had crawled out
of like a scarecrow, black as night, when there wasn't any more
day left behind ever, my all-too-alone-crazy uncle would say,
and I would feel the big bus bump over the road as we played
Gin Rummy and sometimes even Jacks or Better where the
light was small on the itchy fuzz brown bus seat, when I could
not see any more exactly the where-we-were-going-to through

the round-cornered window of things in the dark, and my out-of-the-coal-mine uncle would say then that he was sick of pulling no-good-to-himself-a-damn clubs or hearts or whatever would be no good to him to pull that game, tired of me pulling always the Jack on him, and Jesus-to-Jack-Christ tired of looking at my crooked face crooking him black, and that he was good for only Paso Robles, fold, or no-can-open, and that if I had eyes to tell an Indian from a two-pump gas station, then I could go ahead and pull the yellow string down for the bus driver to stop, to go ahead and stop and drop us crooked Jacks in front of the Injun Hut, near the black as night grape-grown-around farmhouse where God's gopher had crooked him back into the hole—Paso Robles, fold and no-can-open, Sonny, bust as a scarecrow in another man's shirt, my out-of-the-coal-mine uncle would say, and for me to go ahead and pull the yellow string down if he fell asleep, unlikely or even if he didn't, to go ahead and pull the string when I saw a pink Indian with a feather and a log cabin underneath, down for the crooked bus driver to stop this goddamn barrel going and let us out, my uncle said, out to gravel over to that good Injun's hut to see what piss-water they got pissed out that night, scare-crow special, my all-too-alone-crazy uncle would say, and that he had a few stiff feathers left in his pocket to give to the good Indian to go ahead and crook him good, the way God had already crooked him black, and take his easy lid right off, like foam swiped off the top of a glass of piss-water, and then my out-of-the-coal-mine uncle would reach into his pocket and give me a couple of flapjack dollars for the store in the morning, saying that he but probably did have some Mulligan left, enough for us and the dog, and for certain, bacon hung up on the nail, and my uncle would give me the two quarters I liked to give over to the red-and-black-checkered-shirt man with the mustache like Buffalo Bill, who was the bartender—the two quarters it took to get the Eskimo Pie that the red-and-black-checkered-shirt Buffalo Bill man kept down in a black-topped freeze box next to the ice cube bin with the necks and tops of

bottles I could just see, sticking up in it, and a quarter extra
to play cowboy songs with on the red-and-blue-lit-up jukebox,
and then my out-of-the-coal-mine uncle would reach up and
turn off the baby bulb light and say it was no use anyhow to
crawl out of any hole that God held up high the lid to and that
even a dumb gopher knew that, and I would shuffle back the
cards together in the high seat dark and look to see if the line
was still good on the bent corners of the jacks by the just-
enough changing light of the window, and I would put the box
of cards back into my pocket and take an apple from the paper
bag to hold me over, and bite a tooth window into the skin and
pull a strip off and just hold the piece in my mouth for a while,
thin, like the skin scalp of an apple, and roll it around on my
tongue for just looking long out of the window, and I would
look out under trees at dark set-in places that passed by and
at the dime to nickel to quarter to bowl-size-big lights with
hunked-down cars pushing the round headlights out toward
us, it looked to me, coming dimmer just behind—one or another hunked-down car caught in the beams of the barreling
bus for however many bus-blinded seconds, with the light,
slant on some part of windshield face showing out from under
a hunked-down, pushing-up-closer car roof, that I could see
from the high-up-barrelling-bus window, before it would go
back to dark, before the car would push past the double beam
of bus lights and cut, with a shiny fender stuck forward, back
into the dark, the windshield face or faces, passing us dark-
sided by, and I would look out slant to the window for as far
as I could see ahead around the fuzzy brown seat in front, for
the place set-in from the other side of the road where there
would be ice cream on a stick and a high, shiny, red-topped,
spin-around stool for me to spin around on, with a slow
chicken-walk under high, big trees home to the bump-nose-
stung, chain-choked-up dog always after, and sometimes even
a boost-up crawl through the side bathroom top-pulled-down
window when the back porch door would be uncle-locked, like
my all-too-alone-crazy uncle would say then that he had known

damn well all along that it had been locked, except for the
jackass key that he had jackass left in his button-up shirt pocket
so as not to forget, and that he was just a jackass scarecrow in
another man's shirt, my out-of-the-coal-mine uncle would say,
those times when he would forget the key in a shirt pocket or
when my aunt would find it later, left on the dresser in the city,
when I would be the one to go up and over, good-like-a-
gopher into the no-sound, cold bathroom and step down onto
the toilet seat and be the only sound in the house that I could
hear, me, gopher-quick going through the shade-pulled-down
bedroom, with my uncle walking around on the rock-grinding
rain gravel outside of the house, saying loud to me that I could
hear through the walls and the windows that he was not gone
anywhere away, but still there, and that nothing was going to
get me and not to worry about any dumb kind of dark so long
as he was still kicking, and I would get to the kitchen part of
the house, where it could be lighter just a little through the
shade-pulled-down, lemon tree-shadowed windows, if there
was a light moon out that night, but where the floor sounded
different, where the kitchen linoleum sounded all different out
to the corners, different like there was somebody or something
else on it besides just me, that I could hear, I would say out
to my uncle, maybe over by the stove, or moving in the other
bedroom, that I could only maybe see the dresser-by-the-wall
part of and not see who could be behind the closet door,
pulled out open, so that I could only see a dark door space that
maybe a man was deep back inside of instead, and my out-of-
the-coal-mine uncle would grind the gravel over to a kitchen
window and stand close in front of the window for me to see
what my uncle said was him, for me to see a man-shape bigger
and smaller moving in front of the window with the shade
pulled down, and to hear the voice of my uncle saying that it
was just him there, outside the window, and for me to just go
ahead across the linoleum to the tiny back room, where there
were only a couple of dumb cans of dog food up on a shelf,
and some bacon, strung up on a nail, and not any man who

could be standing there in the little room—to just go over all the linoleum quick and turn the pinch lock on the doorknob so he could come on in and flick on the light to show me that there was not another soul there, and to go do it then, like a good boy, good as a gopher, and not to listen to what was just the dark talking, but only just to him, like I would listen if it was Jesus talking, standing right there in the window where I could see him, big as a scarecrow, with nothing else out there, my out-of-the-coal-mine uncle would say, except his two feet and the dog's—me looking slant out of the round-cornered bus window those times, those times during the long, do-nothing summers when my all-too-alone-crazy uncle would fall asleep with his mouth a little open on the itchy fuzz brown bus seat, saying some words that I could hardly much make out to be able to say afterward what he said exactly, except to be able only to tell my uncle, shoulder-jiggled awake in the high seat dark, that I heard him talking like a scarecrow—me looking out then for a pale pink feather of light, stem-stuck into a curving band, hunked hollow around a high-as-a-chimney nickel Indian's pink glass headful of barrel-deep dark. **Q**

That Was in Another Country, and Besides

It has slowly become my intention to kill off Nicholas, but I try not to think about it. Instead, I often go to the window, which is really a set of French doors that gives out onto a shallow balcony overlooking a long stretch of city street. In fact, it is the longest street in the city, which pleases me. It provides a sense of expansion, every prospect, sudden or familiar, striking the eye with its fine chances of permanence. At night, late, the radio playing, I may stand there alone, arms resting upon the railing, perhaps with a newly lit cigarette, and watch the yellow headlights of cars as they travel past. Mornings, I can see the grocer below unrolling his awning and setting out boxes of fruit. In the summer there are wooden crates of plums and peaches and cartons of berries. Later, these give way to the yellow apples from Normandy, big bins of hazelnuts, and chestnuts for roasting as the snow comes on. Eventually there will be blood oranges from Africa, small and not quite round, with a reddish cast to the skin.

But that is still a long way off. For the moment, we are just between seasons, not yet into the devolutions of autumn, but with summer falling away. The trees continue to shade the pavement, but the leaves are thinning, brown at the edges. If there is a chill in the air, as there often is these nights, I sometimes leave the windows closed and simply stand at the glass. After an evening rain, it beads with water and holds my gaze, which might make me reflective, except that usually I just narrow my eyes until the reflection of the room begins to take shape in the window. Behind me will be the bed with its checked cover, the armoire, where lately the cat has taken to sleeping, the glow of the lamp on the desk. Above the desk, on the wall, there are photos—several—and at the correct angle even they are discernible, luminous squares against the darkened wall on the other side of which Nicholas sleeps. One of them, in fact, shows Nicholas and me, each to one side with the sky spreading between us. That was before, and I cannot remember who took it, or even where we were, but we are grinning and a little disheveled, and maybe Nicholas's head lists toward me. Frequently, this is the pose of Nicholas in photographs.

Usually, however, my eye moves quickly over these objects, beyond the desk to where the door appears, and then, to a corner of the wide hallway that holds together the apartment. It is a pleasant space, all in all, enough room for all hours and for all the moods to which we are subject—salon, study, dining room, bedrooms, a large kitchen, too, with a stove painted red. Lately, though, our space seems smaller. Even Nicholas, in his demonic abstraction, has remarked this change. But then, many things have changed in the last year. It is my belief that this started when the men came to fix the noise in the pipes late last November. First, I noticed that we could not keep the house heated, which meant trundling around in sweaters or else living out of sleeping bags. Nicholas, who never minds the cold, continued to walk about in shirt-sleeves and said we should wait and see what happened. After all, it is not our house, he said, but simply the place we rent while we're here. Then the knocking began, vague at first, but slowly localized, like ringing in the ears after one wakes up. Nicholas did not hear it, but I called the heating men anyway. When they arrived they told us that the trouble was not grave, probably nothing more than a leak, but it took them a month or more to complete the work while the apartment went to ruin. For weeks the hallway was strewn with wrenches and drop cloths and odd metal rings. This impinged upon all of us, but on Kafka most of all. He would meow all night long, piteously, as if wounded to the heart, and each morning, he was ill in front of the door to Nicholas's bedroom. By the time the workmen finished, the pipes had been silenced—although the heat has never quite returned—but Kafka was beyond the pale. He may have swallowed some sections of pipe and, in any case, several of his teeth had fallen out. He is an elderly cat, a blue point Siamese to be precise, and admittedly, neither Nicholas nor I are too fond of him. But his sufferings exceed both his physical condition and his ancient sense of rejection. Finally, on the advice of the doctor who lives downstairs, we put him on Valium and that seems to have calmed him. He sleeps a lot now, mostly in my armoire, or sometimes on the bookshelves above the atlases, and he roams the house with only a slightly tormented glaze to his eye. Perhaps soon he will be well.

No use thinking about that, though, and besides, I have already described a good number of things—the view from my window and beyond, the place where I live for the moment, internal, domestic drama and the steady decline of Kafka. But this is because I am unceasingly conscious of the physical world. I feel that it observes me, and I like to watch it back, just in case. I approve of men on corners experiencing air, of the buses carrying people to their destinations, of the way the buildings may tilt in afternoon light—of most everything that I see.

But how shall I describe Nicholas? As a man of elegance, perhaps, in his thought and desire, his way of speech, if nothing else, which is a virtue, but not, of course, a moral virtue— Sade had it, too. But elegance aside as surely it is, still, Nicholas cannot be ignored. He had a way of making himself felt, for example, when we first arrived here, and he would wander around the house muttering "uh huh" all the time. I once knew someone else who had the same habit, but she was very thin and did not count as much. And Nicholas counts, even if now he no longer spends much time around the house. He has a new job across town, and in theory he is always elsewhere, sometimes even after he has come home in the evening. But in practice, he never leaves the apartment any-more. His belongings are everywhere—socks stuffed in corners, keys in the refrigerator, wine glasses on the bathroom sink, stray papers and chewed gum on the table, oceans of books face down on the floor of the kitchen, and especially, amidst everything else, hundreds of uncapped black felt-tip pens poised for the moment when he may need them. Nicholas thinks that he may become a writer, but that explains nothing. Moreover, even if he himself did not have possessions enough to fill up three apartments, he borrows things from me and leaves them about too. I am missing what I need most of the time and cannot get it back, even when I ask. Then there is the humming, humming all the time, as if his life depended upon it, and you may depend upon it, it does. Like a machine inside him droning, the humming never ceases.

Mainly, though, I suppose, there is the question of how he looks—sleek, like a panther, and almost well fed.

In this way, Nicholas takes up all the space. But I can forgive these traits, and do, the humming included, if only because they make for so much life. It is true, too, that objectively speaking, Nicholas may be no larger than anyone else. I have, in fact, spent a good deal of time attempting to measure him against other objects. His shirts are size seventeen, but he is not the sort of person in whose place you might put up even a small building. When seated at a café, he fits snugly behind a newspaper. His feet protrude, but, indeed, they are smaller than most feet, except when he is wearing the cowboy boots we once bought in Mexico. When he naps on his bed, as he often does, his person fits neatly within the bed's perimeter, although there would not be room even for Kafka to lie down next to him. But that is fine, since Kafka has come to prefer the armoire anyway and frequently drools in his sleep. One cannot fault Nicholas for wishing to sleep in peace.

It was not always, either, that he took up more room than I do. If we were walking down the street in afternoon light, the sun behind us as we set out across the city, the shadows that fell at our feet stretched separate before us but equal at every point. They were not precisely the same shape, and yet they were hard to tell apart. Lately, though, I sometimes notice that when Nicholas returns home in the evenings, he seems to loom. It is especially then, in the evening, and more so toward bedtime, that he looms. If we happen to be standing close by in the hallway, before we have turned out the lights, his shadow may fall across me until nothing remains but his familiar outline, arms dangling and tapered toward the hands, head to one side, the shoulders squared. In this way, perhaps, by way of shadow, Nicholas takes up all the space, even as the apartment shrinks around us.

I do not have an expansive character, but neither am I diminished by this turn of events. My feet are well-proportioned, and I take up neither more nor less space than I am supposed to. Still, I have tried to discover imaginative solutions to our dilemma, and, frankly, they have failed. I cannot always be standing at the window in search of some room, especially with the colder weather coming on. By subtle turns, I have also tried to apprise Nicholas of this state of affairs, but he has deployed rather awesome defenses against self-knowledge, and the seasons do not affect him. In fact, very little seems to affect him anymore. This is because he is of a contrary spirit, and it runs against his nature to be affected. It is certain that if asked to get up early, he will sleep dogmatically until noon. When confronted with silence, he will talk in complex clauses like a madman. If the train leaves at three, he insists it means two. No, Nicholas cannot be made smaller simply because I wish it so. But he can be made larger, until even he will have no space. For this reason, I have undertaken a campaign to feed Nicholas until he explodes. I do not know if he will explode entirely, but still, it is possible.

I have not told Nicholas of my plan, which worked well in the early stages. At that point, my efforts consisted in no more than watching him very carefully. Sometimes I wished to tell him of what I knew, but it was enough to realize in solitude that certain foods appeal to him more than others and that with the proper mood upon him, he can be excited to rapturous appetites. Therefore, the expeditions began, from one end of the city to the other, to the street markets by the river on Tuesdays and Thursdays, to the patisserie near the metro, to the fromageries in the 15th. Few people, not even the locals, are aware that the ripest Valencays can be found in the 15th. But I have scoured the city, and by now I have discovered the best of everything and can procure what I need with great efficiency. I have a schedule marked out on a folded paper that I keep in my wallet. It tells me where and when to get what, and in this way I avoid running low on essentials. Never will there come a morning when we are out of bacon, or a dinner that lacks a single ingredient. I have also purchased a great number of cookbooks and several volumes by Robbe-Grillet.

This degree of success alone has made it difficult to conceal my satisfaction from Nicholas. But I surrender no information, and for all he knows, I spend my days as usual, mornings at the café and classes, an afternoon at the book, the two of us at home in the evening. Usually I have prepared most of dinner by the time he returns from work, but there are awkward moments when we stand in the kitchen, exchanging news of the day behind. He may munch some bread that I have carefully left on the counter, and, in the best of moments, he will lift the lids of the pots on the stove to see what we are having. Then I am cheerful. But later, beneath the plates arranged with food and the forks and knives and vases of flowers placed upon the linen tablecloth, beneath the summer light that falls across the room and through the words that float between us, beneath these things, the very table groans with the weight of what I leave unsaid.

It was not always so between us. In fact, much of our time has been organized around the table—three-star lunches of epic proportions, Sunday dinners at the houses of others, decadent breakfasts that last until four. We have discussed the relative merits of sheep and goats, of God and the world, and the migration patterns of the blue-eyed scallop. It travels south in the winter, like birds, but less efficiently. With Dickensian fury we have devoured our way from pea soup through

Stilton and walnuts and across the plains of German philosophy. While deciding upon the state of the soul before birth, we have put away pounds of steak and yards of spaghetti, bowl upon bowl of peaches and cream. We are not particular. When the late shad and asparagus with Hollandaise have given way to bluefish and berries, we have been there in passionate attendance, forks poised lest dinner cool. No fear, and it was at table, too many of them, that Nicholas and I planned our trips, to the Alps, to Algeria, to places we never got to, maps spread end to end, draped over the dishes of butter and cups of cooling coffee. There were afternoons in the marble-topped Russian bar up the street and around the corner, with talk of underground men and plates of borscht, shots of vodka and loaves of black bread. Mornings, then, at wood-topped tables, a café in conversation, and Nicholas would put the world in order while we waited for croissants to arrive with café au lait to wash them down. Do not think, either, that I have forgotten the Margaux and Gigondas and the endless Beaujolais—but it would be futile to enumerate the bottles of wine we have consumed because they defy computation.

Well, there are more staunch soldiers still to die, although, to be sure, there have been setbacks—Nicholas unexpectedly taking sick for a day so that he could eat nothing but Jell-O, or the night that Kafka, in a rage of resentment, leapt from the top of the dish cabinet into the middle of a particularly inspired lamb stew with dumplings. It was too late to prepare something new, and Nicholas went to bed with no more than a bowl of cold cereal filling his belly. The next day, though, life returned to normal and we increased Kafka's dosage of Valium to prevent further mishaps. Of course I suffer, too, somewhat, both in my silence and because of Nicholas's contrary spirit. I cannot eat a morsel, since that is just the provocation he needs to attempt still larger, more rapacious forkfuls. All the while, though, I am no less hungry than ever. I know this because sometimes late at night, after the table is cleared until tomorrow, after the dishes are washed and back in the cabinet, after the sounds of the last "good night" linger and fade in the hallway, then I lie on the bed and feel the pangs. A rumbling emptiness at center that refuses to be wished away. At times I consider a midnight stroll, perhaps to the nearest café for *un sandwich au jambon et un demi,* but that is purely conjectural. Such things have ceased to exist for me. Usually I just wait until I can hear the slow, contented breathing of Nicholas as he sleeps on the other side of the wall. It is comforting to think of him there in the dark, loosely stretched upon the bed, which is not so large after all. He will be dreaming soon, if not already, although it is hard for me to imagine what dreams he dreams. But they do not matter, and I can dream for him; in this way, my pangs are put to sleep.

Besides, no matter how little I sleep at night, in the morning I am as alert as ever, and I will be justified in my efforts. Nicholas's face has taken on a vaguely jowly appearance, at least under certain light, and at times it is possible to imagine that his clothes fall less loosely about him. I have been heartened, too, by his recent purchase of several new shirts. When I checked the collars, I discovered that they are size seventeen as ever, but it is hard to tell with shirts—he may be filling them out with a little more form than before, or he may not. In the meantime, it is hard to avoid noticing that there is less of me all the time. My clothes have begun to hang upon my frame as if upon one of those mannequins you see in the windows of very expensive couturiers. For several weeks I worried that Nicholas might take alarm, but I think that I have been right from the beginning. His abstraction increases by the day, and for every mouthful I forgo, Nicholas grows hungrier and hungrier. It is inexpressibly gratifying to watch him over a plate of double veal chops and noodles as I sit there breaking bread into little pieces and rearranging them in the shapes of trees.

In fact, the project has been proceeding with such success that it hardly fazed me at all when Nicholas announced that he intended to go to Spain for a month. It did throw me into a moderate frenzy, and for several days I left clippings about

Basque terrorists lying around the house. But I could see that opposition was pointless, for his mind can never be changed, despite the dreadful weather they have at this time of year in Spain. Before he left, I packed him a lunch of cold chicken and brownies and boiled eggs, and then we took a taxi to the station together at noon. While we stood on the platform waiting for the train, I surreptitiously sized him up against the passersby and told him about the Spanish chorizos, and black, salted olives, and rough, country wine. He allowed as how such things might be very agreeable, although I know that Nicholas, if left alone, often eats nothing at all. Still, since then a post-card or two has come, and he seems in better spirits than ever. There was a delay in Bilbao because of a porter strike, but he managed to get on with his itinerary just the same, and he says the weather is fine.

It was nonetheless infuriating that Nicholas should leave just when things were going so well. But do not think that in his absence my resolve weakened; indeed, I was subject to religious intensities. My menus attained a degree of extrava-gant invention, until the repasts that I imagined for us upon his return exceeded all bounds of decency. Filet mignons turned into whole sides of beef—fatted calves brought to the altar and reserved for singular destruction. Our time at table grew all-consuming, and Nicholas consumed more and more, as if by an exponential progression. Even after the most sump-tuous of dinners, long after I had gone to bed, he would find himself rummaging in the refrigerator like a man starving in the wilderness. He awoke in the mornings unable to contain himself, bursting into the kitchen with his teeth already in motion. But the explosion would occur by degrees. It came upon him like cramps in the legs, a slow pain that crept from toe to knee to hip and farther up. At first he thought that he had caught the grippe, and he experienced difficulty breath-ing, a tightness in the chest. A light sweat beaded his brow. Because he is obstinate, he refused all medication, never knowing that it could not help in the least. When I would tell

Nicholas that he looked healthier than ever, he fell into fits of hypochondria and requested that I make him chicken soup. In time, he was unable to leave his bed at all.

Later, I would wander about and try to clean up, and then, the matter would be finished.

Being in Spain, Nicholas had no idea about any of these eventualities and doubtless was enjoying plate upon plate of garlic shrimp. In any case, this is merely a skeletal vision. When the moment comes, it will be far grander than even I can conceive. In fact, its very sublimity has somewhat exhausted me. I no longer have the energy to make expeditions, and now that Nicholas is back, I often find it difficult to stay awake through dinner. I nod, and at times I am almost lulled into a state of false remorse. He is ebullient after his trip and seems to have lost no visible substance, but I know that a part of him is missing. In the mornings, walking around the apartment, I may come upon one of his stray socks and feel the sorrow of when he will be gone for good. But that is no more than a kind of nostalgia for a past that still remains in the future, a sense of space that has grown too large because no objects fill it.

It is true that I have lost a sizable amount of weight in the last several months, and that Nicholas himself takes up no more space than before. But for the moment, the apartment is neither larger nor smaller than usual. The books are still open on the kitchen floor, but they can be avoided, and besides, mostly I stay in my room. This means that I cannot cook as much as before, although once in a while I write out elaborate menus on the insides of matchbooks. Later, lying on the bed, eyes closed, I hear the street sounds beyond, know the buildings to be bathed in golden light, life going on below and elsewhere. If the window is open, I can feel the weather turning blue at the edges, the air as it carries another season. When that season comes, I like to think that I may be elsewhere too, in another country perhaps, and in another life.

Lately, I even think about going home, back to the empty American sunlight filling the scene beyond the window. But for now we will stay where we are. Across the street, the grocer is harder at work than ever, moving his endless crates endlessly back and forth, ringing up orders, piling the pears in attractive displays. I have not been to the grocer for a while, but sometimes, if necessary, I do venture out of the house, maybe for a walk down toward the river and across the bridge, or out to the tabac for a packet of Stuyvesant Bleus. There is no one in particular to see, or to speak to, but when I am going in or out I occasionally run into the doctor who lives downstairs. He will take off his hat and inquire after the state of Kafka's health, and then he tells me I am looking too thin. I don't say much to him, but I believe that Kafka has quieted down considerably since his attack on the lamb stew. He may even be aging into a wry kind of wisdom. Q

Boys!

It was as if I heard a hiss come out of my mother, or she was letting me have it some way with air when I said to her *You look so beautiful.*

But she didn't do that.

What she did do was she looked at me.

Maybe not even that, because I was standing—my mouth was at her ear—when I said *You look so beautiful,* so that no one else sitting at the table would hear. Was I whispering because her face had looked to me manhandled, if that were possible, with dips and curves lying pleasingly on her, pleasingly to me on her face?

So what happened then? Because it was *her* turn. Was I pulled away to say something to someone else?

No, I think I sat back down next to her. There was no getting away from her. I had been put there with her for the meal.

But I did not look at her. I was looking to see the shine on my plate rim, the sauce shine on my meal, and I was seeing the beauty of the man next to me, which was so careful in his hair, in his wife's hair that matched his hair, in his wife's pink mouth when she spoke. And with all this beauty going on, my knife, I kept it slicing competently through my meal. I kept it slicing, and I kept putting my knife back into the correct station on the rim of my plate after having sliced.

So when my meal was finished, and I felt that it was finished with no trouble, I got up and I left the people at the table. It must have been just for a moment when I got up, which was to go to the commotion why I finally got up, not to leave my mother—because I am a mother, too, and the commotion was my problem, my children, a disorganization.

My children were going around and around the table. I

think that they were going so fast that I could not have caught the sleeve of even the youngest, even if I had tried reaching out for it. I think, maybe, I did try reaching out for it. But perhaps I didn't.

They all must have been waiting for me for what I would do, everyone else at the table—all the grown-up people—but I was just looking at my children, my children going on and on, and their noise was like huge spills to me that kept being sudden and kept pouring.

And it was pleasing to me, *then it was,* in a certain way, the motion and the commotion, the children getting away from me, and I was watching it, and it was all my fault until the time when it would be over, and it wasn't as if anything could be ruined, I didn't think.

Then I called *Boys!* which I thought was loud, but when I hardly heard the word, because it was as if I had sent the word away, when the children hardly heard the word—they must not have—then I knew it must have been very faint out of my mouth, or just loud enough to be just another push of air to send them around again, to keep them going.

Then I saw a little girl, little enough that I must have missed her when she was going around with the boys, someone else's little girl, shorter than my littlest boy, that I did not know.

She must have thought she was so cute. The girl looked full of glee to me, and I was standing there, waiting for some other mother, the mother of the girl I did not know, to stand up and *do* something—because it was clear to me then that this little girl was the cause, that it was *all her fault,* and that she was the one in charge. **Q**

Grace

It's my being with Sandy at the time that gets to me. I tell Bitsy I'm going out to play some B-ball at the rec center, when I'm really heading over to Sandy's place. I don't know, I felt uneasy about carrying on with Sandy anyway, and who wouldn't feel like hell, not being home when this kind of thing happens to your wife. But it's kind of like, being off with Sandy that night, like it was almost me who did it to Bitsy. Which is something I certainly can't tell her, although I wish I could, so maybe she could free me from it. Whatever that means.

I've been trying to get it together to break off with Sandy for months, only it's always a little different once we're face to face, or lying together on her waterbed. Or it used to be. I haven't even had the urge now in about three weeks. I come home and sit down in the living room, and almost any day of the week I can see the whole thing play itself out again, as if I'd been there watching. Furniture falling, Bitsy screaming for me, the knife, the letters.

Which is the other thing. The letters. W-I-N—right there across her chest; eight separate cuts at least four inches long. I didn't even notice they were letters at first, she was too much of a mess. Even with all the blood, I could tell they weren't much worse than surface wounds, but I figured the son of a bitch had just carved on her at random. But when she gets home the next night, I'm helping her put on some lotion they gave us at the hospital, and that's when I realize. I saw the letters, and for one weird moment I thought for sure she must have known. Must have known where I'd been, what I'd been doing when it happened to her. Which was ridiculous. But then I start thinking about the guy who did it. Maybe *he* knew. Maybe he was telling me something. And I try to think of anyone who might know about me and Sandy. Maybe one of her old boyfriends. So the next day I call Sandy from work, but she says there's no one, nobody who'd care anyway. I tell her to think hard, and she finally sighs and says this is pointless, that I'm just becoming obsessed. But I can barely hear because somebody's putting shovels away in the tool room, and I say, "Of course I'm upset!"

She says, "No, Wynn, *ob-sessed,* like preoccupied too much," as if I never heard the freakin' word before. That's the only thing about Sandy. She graduated from the university here, and sometimes she seems to think she's got something over people like me and Bitsy just because of it. Anyway, she keeps insisting the letters don't mean me at all, which I'm perfectly well aware of, but still. She says maybe it was just some pervert saying he'd won. WIN. But I don't buy it. I'd like to think it's just a coincidence, but I don't know.

Anyway, the first night Bitsy is home, I'm sitting on the edge of the bed helping her with the lotion, and that's when I realize. She's got scrapes on her back and shoulders, but right across her chest and all those freckles, these straight little thin line cuts with stitches: WIN. I just stop right there, and the stuff drips off my fingers onto her nightgown. "Bitsy," I say, "you didn't tell me it was letters."

She looks up at me suddenly and tugs her nightgown around her tiny shoulders. "I thought you knew."

"No," I say.

"I mean, the cop, all those people—they talked to you, didn't they?"

She buttons up the top of her nightgown.

"Yeah, but . . ."

I can remember the cop looking kind of strange when I told him my name, then he asked me to spell it. And spell it again. Then later the intern came out to talk. When I asked him about the cuts, he just said there'd be some scarring, never mentioned anything else. "Well, what the hell does that mean, w-i-n?"

"I don't know! I suppose it's because I was yelling for

you." She starts pulling at a loose thread in the quilt and won't look up.

"Jesus, Bitsy, why didn't *I* know about this?" I kick one of her clogs against the wall, and this palm branch Bitsy brought home from church last month drops off the mirror onto the floor. I leave it there and sit on top of the hamper.

After a while Bitsy sits up and says, "Will you pick that up, please? Anyway, what's it matter? Now you know. It's not as if it happened to you."

"What's that supposed to mean?"

"Just what I said," she says. "I mean, it's not something else we need to worry about, is it?" She reaches for the glass of 7-Up I put on the nightstand for her and takes a slow, delicate sip, barely moving her head to the glass; the son of a bitch wrenched her neck in addition to everything else.

I put the palm branch back on the mirror and go over to the bureau where the phone is, trying to remember the cop's name.

Bitsy sets her glass down and says, "Oh, baby, what are you doing with the phone book? Who are you calling?"

"That cop—or the doctor. I'm your goddamn husband, Bitsy—they should've told me about this."

"Wynn, put the phone down. They were perfectly decent men—please don't go and embarrass me."

" 'Perfectly decent men,' huh? I'd like to know what the hell was so special about them."

"Shut up, Wynn. Just shut up." That's what she tells me. "Give me the lotion, I'll do it myself."

So that's her first night home. By that point I'm almost inclined to head back over to Sandy's, but that's the last place I'm going to now. I tell Bitsy I'm sorry, kick off my sneaks, and sit up on the bed next to her, just holding her. Her hair's still damp from the bath, and her nightgown smells like the cloves from her underwear drawer. She rubs at the patch on my jeans, but then she stops and just stares off at the ceiling light.

After a while she starts pulling at her eyebrows and flicking them onto the floor. I can tell from the way her mouth is set so tight that she's trying to keep herself from crying. I pull her to me and stroke her hair, and pretty soon we fall asleep like this, the lights still burning, me in my clothes, both of us lying on top of the quilt.

A few hours later Bitsy wakes up breathing hard, her eyes darting around the room, like she's done almost every night for three weeks now. It's getting to be a regular ritual, though I think she'll get over it eventually. When I first came back from Nam, I used to hit the dirt every time a car backfired or a balloon burst, but after a while they get to be cars and balloons again.

The next day Bitsy insists on going to work, so I hang around the house till about eight-thirty and take her down to the bank myself. She's a senior teller at the main downtown branch, but her friend Lydia is trying to get her into the loan department, which would be more or less a promotion.

I'm transplanting gladiolus bulbs that morning in the beds on the main campus. Except for a couple of lazy work-study kids, it's all older men who work with me. Around noon I tell Rupert, the only dependable one of the bunch, to make sure everyone's got something to do, because I have to go downtown for some snakes.

The little shop Sandy owns is right nearby, so when I finish up at the toy store I head over to her place. She's had this artsy card and gift shop for about three years—pretty successful apparently, and already she plans to expand. The place is empty when I go in, and I can tell she's surprised to see me. She says hello in a very concerned tone, then leans over for a kiss. I glance out the window and give her a quick one; Bitsy works about three blocks from here.

Sandy's hair looks like she's been toying with it again. She's got a sort of frizz these days, or a perm, something, I don't know. Anyway, I don't really like it, although her hair's a nice dirty blond color, and still comes down to about her shoulders. She's a lot taller than Bitsy, with high cheekbones and the sort of stunning, blue-eyed look you can't ignore in a bar—at least I couldn't. She broke her nose diving off some-body's boat a couple years back, and you can sort of tell, it goes off to the left a little, but somehow it only makes her more attractive.

She asks right away how Bitsy's doing, and I tell her not too bad, that she went to work this morning.

"That's a good sign," Sandy says. Then, "What's in the bag?"

I open it and show her.

"Snakes?"

"Keeps the birds away when we put new seeds down."

She raises her eyebrows, as if to tell me it sounds pretty unlikely, but I let it go. She takes my hand in both of hers and says, "You don't look too good, you know. You're still blaming yourself for things, aren't you?"

"What do you expect me to do?"

"I expect you to let up on yourself," she says. "You're going to drive yourself nuts."

"Sandy, you don't just bury this kind of thing and forget about it."

"Look," she says, and she straightens her little credit card machine, "it happened, Wynn. It would've happened if you'd been playing basketball or out buying snakes. It would've hap-pened anyway."

"That's a stupid attitude," I tell her. Because if I'd really gone to the rec center, I'd have been home by nine-thirty. At the hospital the cop had asked Bitsy whether she remembered what time it all started, and what room she'd been in earlier. She told him she was ironing shirts in the bedroom, that the nine o'clock movie had only been on a little while when she heard the knock at the door, which she thought was me, that I forgot my key again. Then when Bitsy is getting X-rayed the cop asks *me* questions, including where *I'd* been. I didn't know if I should be straight with him, and expect him to keep it under his hat, or what. I finally just told him I was playing basketball with some buddies, and then *I* start feeling like some kind of criminal.

"Wynn, you keep on like this, you're going to resent me and Bitsy both. You've got to ease up on yourself," she tells me. But what else is she going to say? She wants me to leave Bitsy and cut out this see-you-when-I-can crap, so of course she's got to seem like some sort of merciful angel.

I don't know, I just think I liked it a lot better when things were more casual between us. I can remember back in the winter, lying in bed talking at Sandy's one Saturday afternoon. I asked if it bothered her that I was married, and she said, "No, not really, kind of makes it more exciting." But lately it's like she's trying to push Bitsy out of the picture all the time. On one level I think she's sincere about all this concern for me, but a lot of times it's as if she's just trying to seem nicer than Bitsy. Not that she even knows Bitsy—she says she went into the bank to get a look at her once—but she tries to badmouth her a lot, and used to say things like "Where's Bitchy tonight?" which really pissed me off, even when I was mad at Bitsy anyway.

"Listen, sweet," Sandy says, and sticks her finger in between the buttons of my work shirt. "We'd better do some talking about this soon, because you sure as hell can't talk to *her* about this one. And you're going to go bonkers if you keep it bottled up."

It seems so stupid to be talking about me like *I* need help, when if she could have seen Bitsy bolting out of a sound sleep last night . . . I don't say anything, and Sandy laces her fingers with mine on the counter. "I'm glad you called me Tuesday night," she says. "I mean, that you felt like you could talk with me about it."

I wish she wouldn't say this, because it reminds me of just what a bastard I am for calling her while Bitsy was lying in the hospital. Also, listening to Sandy's scratchy voice saying these things and watching the little points her nipples make against that dark purple blouse, I can feel a little life down there for the first time in days. "Yeah, maybe we can talk," I say. "Not here, though."

"Tonight?"

"Not tonight, okay? I can't leave her alone. Soon."

A lady with a kid comes into the store and nods at us. "I'll call you," I tell Sandy, and head for the door. She gives me that sad, pleading look, like won't I stay, and I feel sort of good on Bitsy's account for leaving.

That night Bitsy and I are lying across the bed watching TV, and in the middle of the local news there's this commercial for the state lottery. The TV screen shows a roulette wheel going round and round, and in each place where there'd usually be a number it says WIN. No shit. Makes me uneasy as hell, almost before I even know why, and I can imagine what it does for Bitsy. I take her hand and squeeze it, and she rolls her eyes at me.

The phone rings, and my stomach knots up a bit worrying that it's Sandy. "I'll get it," I say, but it's only Bitsy's mother checking in. I don't think her parents hold anything against me for being out the other night, though I can just imagine Joyce asking Roger what the hell I was doing out playing basketball so late. Mostly we get along pretty well, though. Bitsy and I have been together since tenth grade, and sometimes it's almost like Joyce and Roger are my own folks, though of course you never forget they're in-laws. Especially Joyce.

From what Bitsy's saying, I can tell her mother's asking her if maybe she wants to go and talk with Father Macklin at St. Joseph's, which apparently she doesn't, and I think that's just as well. Not that I have anything against priests. I knew a few decent ones when I was younger, including the guy who first showed me that gardening is a lot more than just flowers and dirt. But all this laying family problems and relationship problems at some priest's feet I can't go for. Okay, maybe the guy knows spiritual things, but there's a kind of knowledge that comes from living with a woman day after day that a lifetime wanker just can't know about.

Anyway, Bitsy is saying, "I know Father Macklin's dealt with these kinds of things, but I don't *need* to talk with him. Mom, I just won't, okay? I've got Wynn if I need to talk." She finally tells Joyce we'll be over for dinner Friday night, and eases herself back onto the bed. She's still pretty sore, and she's got some mean-looking bruises on her arms. I turn the TV off and ask, "How's your mom?"

"Okay," she says, but I don't think Bitsy is really listening. She's just lying back, staring at the ceiling, pulling at her eyebrows and grinding them between her fingers. She's still dressed up from work, wearing these navy blue pumps with straps. I'm about to take them off for her to make her more comfortable—she doesn't like shoes on the quilt—but I think of how that son of a bitch must have pulled her clothes off her the other night, and I don't even want her making the association.

A car honks next door, and I remember the stuff I left out in the back seat. "Be right back," I say, and I get up from the bed and pull on my sneaks.

Bitsy sits up. "Where are you going?"

"Just out to the car."

She sits there frozen, looking at me kind of panicky.

"Really," I say. "I'm just going to get something from the car—I'll be right back."

The rear door of the Toyota, where I got sideswiped last year, gives its goddamn groan and I grab the five roses wrapped in muddy newspaper from the back seat. They were the first ones to come up in the bed next to the president's house, and I figure Bitsy can use them a whole lot more than those folks. There's no vase in the kitchen, but there's this empty Mrs. Butterworth's maple syrup bottle up on top of the fridge, shaped like somebody's grandmother in an apron. I peel the label off, clip the stems, and fill the bottle up to the old lady's neck with cool water; with the five roses, it actually looks pretty good.

Heading back to the bedroom, I sing "Red Roses for a Blue Lady"—but when I get to the door, Bitsy's got her face in the pillows, and her shoulders are heaving. I feel like a fool. "What's wrong?" I ask.

"Nothing, I'm okay," she mumbles.

"Come on, Bits. Were you thinking about it again?"

"No, I wasn't," she says, "but look at me." Her voice sounds pathetic and little girlish. "Twenty-seven years old and I'm afraid to be in the house by myself. How am I going to live like this? You can't stay and babysit me every time you want to go out. But I *don't* want to be here alone."

I tell her she won't have to be, and massage her back till she stops crying.

After a bit, she turns over a little, facing me again, and rubs at her cheek. "Also," she says, "you sort of blame me for it, don't you, Wynn? For what happened."

"What do you mean?"

"I just think maybe you hold something against me for it. Like the thing you said about that doctor the other night. You're just so far away all the time. Always spacing out, like you don't want to be with me or something."

"Bitsy, I don't blame you."

"I don't mean you really *blame* me. But he was going to kill me, Wynn."

She pulls a handkerchief out of my back pocket and dries her nose. She looks pathetic now, pieces of her hair all wet and matted to her cheeks. I pull her head onto my lap as gently as I can, but she starts crying again, wiping her cheek on my leg. "Bitsy, really, I know you did all you could. It's okay," I say.

"Yeah, all right," she tells me. She rubs her eyebrows, which look rashy and patchy from where she's always pulling at them. "But I really feel bad, Wynn. I mean, bad for me, but also for you, you know? That I couldn't stop him."

"I know you do," I say. "I know it."

I don't see Sandy for a few weeks, but then one Monday morning Bitsy says she's going back to her meditation class after work, and Lydia wants to take her out to dinner afterward. So Monday afternoon I call Sandy and tell her I'll meet her at her place that evening.

I get there, and I'm barely inside the door when Sandy wraps her arms around me, a real pelvic sort of hug, which I don't feel very sincere returning. She touches the tip of her tongue to the end of my nose, which she says is sunburned, and goes to get me a beer. She's wearing this gauzy white blouse and a pair of old Levi's that fit her almost like a second skin and her red cowboy boots. I toss my fatigue jacket on the sofa and sit down next to it.

I like the way Sandy's got her place decorated—lots of plants, walls full of pictures, a big loom trailing colorful yarns in one corner. Above the sofa she's got these three black-and-white photographs of her brother carrying a bushel basket of leaves, and he's laughing a little bit more in each one.

I pick up a copy of *Rolling Stone* from the coffee table, and start reading this thing about Agent Orange, which as far as I know I never got exposed to, but who knows? Sandy is standing in the kitchen mixing a glass of red zinger. She says, "Are you reading, or talking to yourself?" That's her way of telling me she doesn't like the fact I sometimes move my lips when I read. "I'm just asking myself why you buy this crap," I say. She brings me a bottle of Tuborg and sits sideways on my lap, asking how long I can stay.

"Only for an hour or so," I tell her.

She scowls and makes a disappointed *dit* sound with her tongue.

I don't know if Sandy really thinks I'm some kind of prize, or if she's just gotten to be thirty-one and now she's worried about being single all her life. I first started seeing her when things were a little rough with Bitsy back in the winter, but not that bad, no worse than the problems everybody's got. I was drinking a lot, which Bitsy doesn't like, and maybe her nagging just gave me a good excuse to spend time with someone else.

"Well, can we at least go lie down?" Sandy says.

"I guess."

"Oh, you sound real enthusiastic."

"Jesus, Sandy."

"Well, maybe I need a little more attention. I'm sick of just being somebody's monthly diversion," she says, giving me the very opening I need to take this conversation where I think it should go.

Because something's got to change. I move through every day now feeling distracted, as if something's incomplete or out of place. It got to the point where I finally called the rectory at St. Joseph's one morning, to see when this new priest was hearing confessions, but when the time came I didn't do it. It wouldn't make any difference in the end, some stranger giving the same routine he mouths for every other kneeling nitwit. What good would that do me? So I never went, and I don't mention it to Sandy, either. I don't know, it's like, sometimes you want another woman to be sort of a buddy, almost like one of the guys, but they always want to be a wife instead.

Bitsy and I watch TV that night, and there's this great relief that comes from breaking with Sandy, although something's still not back in place. Even so, I go to bed that night feeling more relaxed, and Bitsy and I fool around a little for the first time since it happened. Bitsy's cuts are healing pretty well; the scars are probably going to look like five lines—the downstroke cuts—instead of letters now. Things seem a little better all week, but not better enough, and I still can't always look Bitsy in the eye. Also, she's still full of nervous habits, and wakes up most nights for no reason.

Last night—Friday—we did some grocery shopping, and

after dinner I got drunk just sitting watching this detective movie on TV with Bitsy. Later on in bed, I start feeling sick, the room's doing its circle routine, and Bitsy wakes up as I'm heading for the bathroom. But before I can get around the bed, my stomach starts somersaulting, and a corner of the quilt gets covered. Bitsy's real good about it—changes the sheets while I'm in the can, brings in a bucket, and sets a damp washcloth on my forehead once I'm back in bed. She ought to be mad, but she just holds me and whispers nice things, which means a lot at that point.

This morning—Saturday—there's no hangover, miraculously, but Bitsy didn't get much sleep on account of me, and she's still lying in bed. I haven't even got a headache, so I sweat through a set of push-ups, and I can smell last night's gin breaking through the pores on my arms. I lie back on the rug after fifty, and something's still eating at me.

I remember the first time I was seeing another woman, years ago, feeling like I should tell Bitsy after I broke it off. Maybe that was because I thought she'd find out anyway, though, since it was a neighbor. But I never told her, and she never found out. The guilt just dried up, and I realized soon enough that was the thing to do—swallow it. But this isn't just the fling with Sandy that's eating me. It's been almost three weeks since it happened to Bitsy, and I'm certainly not operating on normal, which isn't helping Bitsy get any better, either. She knows something's wrong, and I have a feeling she still thinks I blame her.

I think again about my idea of going to confession last week. I'm not usually that religious—Bitsy gets me to go to mass at Christmas and Easter, and sometimes on just a regular Sunday. I used to pray a lot when I was in Nam, more out of loneliness than being afraid most times, but this was the thing: without even thinking about it, just spacing out on some stretch of road, or lying against a couple of sandbags at night, my prayers would always be spoken to Bitsy. Never to God, not dear Jesus or any of that crap, though I know it's not just crap for some. You can laugh, but it was like Bitsy, she was my God. Like everything was in her hands, or she could sort of oversee it all, anyway. Not everyone has someone like that, but like I said, Bitsy and I have been together since tenth grade, and I think maybe if you've got that kind of person, they can do for you what the nuns used to call Grace. There's just this one person who can tell you what you've done is okay, or whose forgiveness is the only thing that matters if it wasn't.

I've got to tone the story down, of course. What really matters is just her knowing where I was, what I was more or less up to when it happened. I tell myself I'm not going to run around anymore after this, but who knows what's going to happen a few years down the road, and I'm not even sure I really hope it deep down. But one thing I do know is that parts of those letters are always going to be there when Bitsy's getting dressed in the morning, or when we go swimming in the summer, getting in bed at night, you name it. And she's the one person who could make that a fact I can live with. She's lying in bed still, reading *People* magazine, which just came in the mail, and I go and kneel down by the bedside and put my face in her lap. She closes her magazine slowly and sets her hand on my head like a blessing. **Q**

Ready, Almost Ready

There was a newspaper column in the sports section, and it told about the big catch of each day. Roebuck was the outdoor editor, and he had a corner reserved for the lucky fisherman's picture. Bass fishermen were featured in the "Lucky Corner," for there was a bass lake nearby, and it was, more or less, a bass town. In fact, it was a bass state.

It was the state of Mississippi.

What little money there was, was often spent on boats, and fish finders, and trailers, and also on ugly, hideous purple worms, which were made of a greasy plastic and manufactured in a foreign country.

Roebuck had been watching the lake—the Ross Barnet Reservoir—for several years, as he worked on the "Lucky Corner" column, and he knew that justice was not being served; the lucky fisherman whose picture ran each day was not the real winner.

There was an old man, a lunatic—ninety-four years old—and he was the one who was really making the big catches, almost every day. He was a witch, Roebuck thought, was how he did it. He was magic.

The old man's name was Jorro, Roebuck knew, because that was what was painted, crooked and in white paint, on the side of his battered, aluminium canoe, out of which he fished daily.

He fished out in the center of the huge lake.

Roebuck hid in the bushes and watched, all the time, with a spotting scope, as the old man caught fish. He caught fish in June, and in July, and in August. The old man wore nothing but a loincloth and greased himself up with baby oil before casting out. He looked like a seal. He looked like a catfish.

He used crawdads for bait.

Roebuck was an aficionado of B.A.S.S. T.O.U.R.N.A.M.E.N.T.S.

What he saw out on the lake, an old man having fun, somehow troubled him.

He felt as if the old man was somehow scorning his newspaper, even scorning Roebuck's way of life, by never showing up with his prize catches to have his picture taken for the "Lucky Corner," to claim the weekly twenty-five-dollar cash prize.

What Jorro was catching, out there, was catfish. He was catching them from a depth of one hundred feet.

The fish he was landing were as large as he was.

Sometimes Roebuck would watch, through his spotting scope, and would not believe what he was seeing. It got him all hot and bothered.

Jorro would throw down his paddle when he had one, and would tie the clothesline off and pull it in, hand over hand, fighting the great fish, coiling the line in by hanks and then, like someone from an old Tarzan movie, the old man would throw a leg over the wet fish when he had it at the surface, and with a scissors hold he would wrestle it into the bottom of the boat. Both of them would thrash around in there for quite some time, unseen: the sound of bumps, and elbows. Sometimes the great fish's head would rear up, like a Chinese dragon's, mouth gaping, eyes bulging—and then Jorro's arm would pull it back down again, and the fight would continue.

Jorro had a small pistol, a .38, and the catfish that were too wild to subdue, or too big to fit on the stringer, he would shoot in the head as if they were wounded deer. Then he would run a lasso through their gills, ease them overboard, and paddle in slowly, towing the fish behind, with the fish's great pale swollen belly bobbing, like another smaller—though not much—boat.

The water-skiers that frequented the reservoir would buzz

him, circling around and around him, as he made his slow way in, but the old man never seemed to notice.

Some trips, Jorro would stay out on the lake for three, four, five days and nights: fishing with a lantern at night and listening to the radio and dozing in the stupefying heat. The water would be still, and locked into flatness; the sun so fierce, in Mississippi, that not even the water-skiers ventured out onto the lake at straight up noon.

But a hundred feet down, it was nice and cool.

It was as if the old man had been there, to know what it was like, to know how to fish it, that deep, thought Roebuck.

Roebuck had been watching the old boy for five summers. Jorro used a volleyball for a bobber and wadded the crawdads onto a monstrous hook as big as a man's foot.

A smarty-pants bait fisherman, Roebuck thought.

It had to be terribly hot, out there on the water like that, with no cap, no sunglasses, not even an umbrella, and Jorro stayed out there until he caught a fish; whatever it took, however long.

Roebuck stayed too, when he could, and watched.

There was a sort of catfish fan club that the old man had, as best as Roebuck could tell. Jorro's old truck had Copiah County license plates, which meant that he was from the hottest, most wretched part of the state, where there were not even really towns, just communities that masqueraded as such. They had a zip code, but no post office. They didn't have a newspaper, or a dentist, or even a grocery store.

They just *lived* out there, in the woods. Roebuck distrusted them. They did not belong to the fishing clubs. They did not use lures. They did not fish in the bassathons.

Sometimes Jorro's fans would come watch. He was a hero to them, it was easy to see. Copiah County was thirty miles away, and yet somehow they seemed to all know when he was about to catch a big one. They would begin to arrive, driving

their old trucks and blasted-out cars without mufflers, sounding like an invading army, and bringing with them their babies
and their grandparents and picnic baskets. Entire generations
of Copiahnites would show up, and when a festive number of
them had assembled, Jorro would hook a big catfish. Sometimes the fans would show up in the blinding bright dead-ass
middle of the day, Roebuck had noticed, and other times, at
the soft cooling end of dusk, when fireflies were beginning to
blink. They just knew when to be there. They were all magic,
Roebuck thought. Witches, all. He stayed motionless in the
bushes and watched, knowing in the yellow fatness of his heart
that if they were to discover him, they would sacrifice him to
the lake, roast him on a spit, and dance as he screamed. It was
the way witches were, he knew, and Roebuck was frightened
of them.

The water-skiers whizzed around Jorro, waved and
pointed and hooted at his canoe, and at the pole—a skinned,
green sapling—in his hands, because it was so hot, so hot. It
seemed to be melting the water, so great was the heat.

But a hundred feet down, thought Roebuck, a hundred
feet down, it was drafty, and icy.

The town, the villagers, would be waiting, and watching.
They would be quaffing beers and cooking hot dogs, waiting.
And when Jorro would hook one, everyone knew it. The really
big fish—a hundred-and-thirty, a hundred-and-forty pounds—
would start dragging his canoe across the open lake. Jorro
would set the hook, tie the line off, and if the fish was too big
to pull up, he would start paddling for shore with it. He would
start singing his fish-catching song, too, the one without any
consonants in it. Slick with sweat, Jorro would dig at the water
furiously with his paddle, singing and chanting, and the villagers would line the shore, waving him in.

He would get it into the shallows—the top half of the big
fish's head rising up above the water, bewildered, whiskers
sprouting from its head like wild lilies—and like savages,

Jorro's villagers would drop their beers and charge out into the shallow water and wrestle the slick and muddy fish into final submission; beating and kicking the fish, they would drag it up onto the shore and up the hill and under the pine trees.

Roebuck watched, with wide eyes. Jorro and the villagers would fall back and lie down in the grass and good-smelling pine needles, gasping like the fish, and Roebuck knew that the slight breeze that is always moving through a stand of pine trees had to feel good, as it passed over their wet shirts, their soaked denims, Jorro's leopard-spotted loincloth.

They closed their eyes and tried to catch their breath. Sun came through the branches and landed in patches on their cheeks, their shoulders. Children circled the fish, moved in, and touched it, with their fingers.

The catfish would be leaving this world, but it would be cool, under the pines, and as his big gills flapped slowly, quietly, he would look almost content—his yellow belly looking as if he had swallowed a bag of horse feed.

And children would pour water on him, to keep him alive, while the men rested.

They were all magic, Roebuck thought. They were all witches. Greasy, ugly, nasty brown catfish. Roebuck wanted Jorro off the bass lake, but he did not know how to do it.

Sometimes Roebuck had nightmares about the catfish, and dreamed that with their round little unblinking gold eyes, they were watching him as he slept, and that with their long, droopy whiskers and slightly obscene grins—like Jorro's grin, whenever the old man first hooked into one, the tongue hanging slightly out—they were laughing at him. And Roebuck would dream, too, that the sheets covering him were a catfish's mouth, swallowing him, pulling him down, farther down, into a place where he would never again be able to write the "Lucky Corner." A place where, like the catfish, Roebuck would never again see light: just a pale, fuzzy shimmering, far above, marking where he had once been, where once there had been light and sun.

Catfish were Satan's little schoolchildren, Roebuck thought.

Catfish were nasty little harbingers of evil.

And when they got to be the size that Jorro was catching, they ate Roebuck's beloved bass!

Roebuck watched Jorro all through the next summer. It was then Jorro's ninety-fifth year, and Roebuck could tell that the old man was getting cocky. He had started sprinkling salt and pepper on the surface before dropping his hook overboard. And some days he invited old ladies to go out in the canoe with him, as many as he could fit, and they would be all dressed up in their Easter dresses, wearing sun hats, excited, holding bouquets of flowers, and the old ladies would watch the water closely as if searching for the fins of circling sharks. They would be in a sort of frenzied ecstasy, so great was their delight at being, for a day, free of the nursing home, and they would all be wearing orange kapok life-preservers. And they would have little fans, like the ones funeral parlors passed out on hot days during the service—square cardboard cutouts, with pastel Bible scenes, attached to a popsicle stick—and they would all be fanning one another with them, and whenever Jorro caught a catfish, they would fan him too, to keep him cool, as he wrestled and struggled.

One time he spilled them and overturned the canoe, so great was his fish, but all of the old women had on their life-preservers, and they bobbed in the lake like spilled fruit, and screamed forlornly. But Jorro swam them in, saved them, one by one, swimming with a wiry arm locked around their necks, dragging them in, like a mother otter with kits. And the water was hot as he swam.

Roebuck watched, fascinated.

But made no move to help.

Jorro made several trips, and laid the old women, in their

colored and polka-dotted dresses, out on the beach like towels, to dry in the sun.

The old women slept, exhausted by the near-drowning, and then, slowly, began to awaken, yawning and stretching, and rubbing their eyes.

The old man was everybody's hero.

Roebuck had lost his job, because of his inattention to it. But still he continued to spy. It was hot in the bushes. He had one of those little battery-operated hand-held fans, and he would swelter in the bushes as he squinted through the spotting scope and directed the little fan's breeze onto the back of his neck, his furry forearms, which had bits and pieces of twig and leaf caught in them. It was so hot. He was getting fat, as big as a barrel, and had become addicted to drugs. Sometimes, he would stuff his underwear full of the plastic worms, just from boredom. He had beers with him, in a little ice chest, and he would drink ten of them, twelve, fourteen at a time, as he watched.

All through that ninety-fifth summer, Jorro caught catfish. He laughed each time he hooked one. Roebuck pawed the sweat from his eyes and squinted, trying to figure out what was making the old fool so happy. It was so hot. Roebuck felt faint with disillusionment that he was not a hero, that he had saved neither drowning old ladies nor himself. He staggered out onto the beach and stuck his fingers in his ears and made garbled, pig-grunting sounds. There was some mud where the lake had dropped from the dry hot summer, and Roebuck peeled his wet T-shirt off and skinned out of his hot boxer shorts and ran and jumped in it.

He slid around in the mud like a fat salamander.

"Bassin' for dollars!" mad Roebuck shouted, making swimming motions in the mud. "Bassin' for dollars!"

The sun was brutal, straight up and stunningly bright, and Jorro, though he could not see what was making all the commotion, seemed to know, and without turning his head, he pulled up his line, and paddled a little farther out into the center of the lake, a little farther away from the noise, and he let out some more line, to go deeper.

The radio played, static and crackle, occasional words.

The old man lit a cigarette and kept his back to the shore. The sun was as bright, he knew, as death was dark. He sat there sweating, and watched the white blaze of his volleyball, and the sun, shining off the water and into his eyes, and he tried to memorize just exactly how bright it all was, how bright and warm, as if storing it up in his mind for when he would want to remember.

He smoked and scratched his shoulder occasionally, and thought what a good time he was having.

He wanted one more.

Each one, each time, made the old man want the next one just a little more.

The water-skiers whizzed past—riding the wake, a girl and a boy in tandem, both of them golden-haired and bronzed, the girl in a yellow bikini. They were waving at the old man, shouting something, giving him the thumbs-up signal.

They raced past his canoe, nearly swamping it they came so close, and flashed great white smiles. The girl had large bosoms, like pillows, and she winked, and then zoomed back across the wake, away from him, moving so fast that she might have been fired from a cannon.

Jorro smiled and waved after them and took out another cigarette, sprinkled a little more salt and pepper on the water's surface once his boat had stopped rocking, and let out another ten feet of clothesline.

He would go a little deeper.

Slowly, he lowered his hook into the place where there wasn't any light.

He rubbed his face, as if sleepy, and hoped the girl would come back, maybe let go of the rope and glide in to where he was fishing.

Lately, the old man had been captured by the idea that

when he got to be a hundred, it would all start over again. Everything. It was August. Dragonflies circled his boat in the heat, in the brightness, and dabbed the water with their stingers. He blinked.

It was all so bright. **Q**

Chinese

Brian sits with his hands under the table, fingers up-turned like legs of dead beetles. He'd like to say something to Brenda, but she has moved her chair away—the leg of the table was between her legs. It would be better if she could scoot toward him, even if he had to move closer to Mrs. Benjamin. The distance between them is disconcerting. Only their butter plates meet. Brenda rearranged them to give Laura room. Laura is at the end of the table with almost no space to plant her elbows. Girls Laura's age plant their elbows in public, whenever they can, as an act of defiance. Mrs. Benjamin can't see Laura's elbows or her dress shoes kicked off under the table; otherwise there would be Young Lady This and Young Lady That. How people continue to be families Brian doesn't know.

"Brian, would you like some shrimp?" Mrs. Benjamin's face is too near his. He leans to one side, toward the vacant space. Brenda is eating shrimp almost daintily. Really, she's picking at it, unconvinced she wants to eat it. He knows her. The side of her head is waiting for him. He must answer Mrs. Benjamin. Over my dead body, he thinks. Brenda's hair twitches.

"Okay," he says.

"It's very good," says Mrs. Benjamin. "You won't regret it."

Why would he regret eating a shrimp or two, a pear slice or two? She's condemning his skinniness.

"Leave him alone. The worst thing you can do to a teen-ager is watch him grow."

Who said this? Probably the woman who's talking to Connie, nodding her silvery head. Joan? Mrs. Seymour? Brian can't remember her name. He's not the sort of young man who would interrupt a conversation to ask someone's name. Jane?

"My son's a walking catastrophe." Mrs. Seymour glances sideways at Brian, and something freezes, for one moment, the side of her face. "All I know is, he won't do anything desperate."

"You're so calm, Jane. How do you know? The teachers say Tony needs regular counseling."

"Educators!" Mrs. Seymour chokes, spits a fleck of ice across the table. The candle flame hisses and cracks. "Faith. That's how."

Mrs. Seymour's dinner companion shifts in his chair. He's over six feet tall and even quieter than Brian, more suited to silence.

Brian's thoughts are slippery maggots, his face a puzzle of movement. It's easier, he decides, to remember men's names. The man with Mrs. Seymour is Gary Hansen. He used to play baseball.

Mrs. Seymour takes Gary's hand.

"Where is the bathroom?" Brenda is asking someone— where is the bathroom?

"Over there." Laura admits vaguely that she's not sure.

"I'll find it."

Don't go! Brian thinks so loudly he's afraid he's said it.

Brenda disappears, following Mrs. Cherry, the wife of the restaurant proprietor.

Mrs. Benjamin flips her fingers as a silencing gesture at her husband.

"What, dear?" Mr. Benjamin talks loudly. Mrs. Benjamin leans forward, the angular shelf of her bosom pushing against her plate.

"*Sss* . . . the . . . supposed to . . . *sss* . . . matter . . . us."

"I don't *know*, Martha. I am sure that if you asked them, they would . . ."

"What time is it?"

Brian tells Tom it is eight o'clock.

Tom is casting about for a new conversation. He considers Gary, the ex-athlete, then leans suddenly toward Brian.

"What did you say you do, Brian?"

Mrs. Seymour's neck lengthens and her eyes dart for plates.

"Oysters?" she says politely.

"Here, Jane," says Tom, reaching in front of Herbert Benjamin. Herbert's dinky dark eyes scrutinize his wife's tight lips. She's mouthing something again.

Brian clutches at linen under the table—the tablecloth scrapes like a skirt across his pants.

"So, what *do* you do?" Tom asks again. Tom asks questions to be asked questions.

"Encode firearms."

"Huh?"

"Serial numbers, keypunching."

"Where were we?" Mr. Benjamin twists in his chair to face Tom. His shoulder juts over the table, a glacial ridge. Jane abandons Connie and vies for a word with the men.

"Dad, Gary and I read that book, and what *we* think . . ."

"Who's Gary?"

"I'm Gary."

"I'm terribly sorry, Gary."

Gary looks blank. Herbert looks certain.

"I met you last month at that cast party. You and Jane came with my grandson."

"I'm afraid not." Gary looks uneasily at Jane.

Jane looks miserably at all of them.

Mrs. Benjamin uncorks a bottle of white wine. "Brian? Your glass is empty." Brian can't tell his glass from Brenda's. He lets her fill both of them. Where is Brenda?

Mr. Benjamin tells a story about losing his passport at the Cairo airport. "Laura was already *on* the plane. So was Brenda's and Brian's mother. The stewards were running around. 'Passport of Ben-ya-meen, Ben-ya-meen passport.'

I'm not kidding. I thought it was *over.* " Mrs. Benjamin twists her watchband. The men and women at the table are laughing.

"Mushrooms," says Mrs. Benjamin. "How's that sauce? This one's good. It reminds me of lemon, but I know it's not."

Brian stands. The edge of the tablecloth goes up with him, clings to his belt buckle, so he must beat it down. Everyone looks at him. The two old ones at the end glare at him, four stupid eyes.

"Where's the bathroom?" Brian asks Mrs. Cherry.

"Down here." She leads the way.

"That's not for you," says Mrs. Cherry. "Yours is over here."

"What I want is . . ."

"You can't go in there. See the dress. Yours has pants. What you want?"

"A girl. Dark hair? Is she in there?"

Mrs. Cherry sizes him up, his crumpled shirt, digital watch. She pushes against the door of the ladies' room. "What's the name?"

"Brenda."

Before the door shuts, Brian glimpses floral walls, rows of light bulbs reflected in a mirror, someone's swinging foot. He sits down on a bench under the pay phone and rolls and unrolls his sleeves.

Herbert Benjamin's voice boxes its way down the hallway: "I'm not saying that people can't read the book, I'm saying it's . . ."

"What are you waiting for?" Brenda stands over him, her chin a little wet.

"Let's get out of here."

"We can't just leave."

"You did," he says.

"Maybe I feel sick. I'm trying to cope, at least."

"I don't like those people."

"Tell them you're an artist. They'll talk to you then."

"Artist?"

Brenda's eyelids thicken and shut. She's counting. "I'm—not—talking to you." She runs back into the ladies' room. Brian imagines tearing off Mrs. Cherry's dress, putting it on, flapping its black and white wings.

Instead, he goes to the men's room. One of the bulbs is burned out. It's cold. The walls are baby blue tile. There isn't even a mirror. He spits in a urinal, tucks in his shirt.

"Brenda, how about you? Here's Brian. Brian, would you like some more?" Mrs. Benjamin is a huge monarch butterfly. She puts turkey and a dab of cranberry on a little painted plate and pushes the plate at Brian. She feeds everyone.

"I'm fine. Thanks, Mrs. Benjamin." He has killed himself in the bathroom. His mind is empty.

"Brenda, some of this?"

"No, really, we're fine."

Mrs. Benjamin shrugs and scrapes the rest of the spinach and all except one carrot onto her plate.

Under the table Brian takes Brenda's hand. Brenda sips from her teacup, but it's empty.

"They're all *out* of sherbet. How disappointing."

"I'm full, anyway."

"Look at you two. Who would think you're brother and sister, the way you get along?"

Mrs. Seymour cocks her head from one side to the other. An ice cube slides between her molars and bulges at the side of her jaw.

"Herbert, a toast?"

"Let's finish this damned wine."

"To health."

"And good reviews."

All the people raise their glasses, clink them and sip.

"Not a late night for me."

"We'll take all three cars."

"Suppose you borrowed one, just for the night?"

"It broke. I couldn't believe it, but it did. It just . . . broke."

Brian moves his arm, and the talking resumes.

"Tomorrow I go."

"All the expectations in the world."

"I've tried, he's still not home."

"Tomorrow then."

"Shall we?"

"Let's."

"Is this anyone's scarf?"

Brenda takes her scarf and plays for a moment with the fringe. Brian lifts her coat from the back of her chair and helps her into it. He touches her sleeve, but she doesn't feel it. Everyone is standing. Everyone faces in a slightly different direction.

The group moves slowly toward the door, buttoning, talking, digging for keys.

"Follow me in the black one."

"Okay. It's cold out there. Zip up!"

Brenda runs ahead of Brian.

She catches up to Laura.

She says something. **Q**

Dear to Whoever Finds This and Reads This So That You Should Know Dozier and Me Are Not All Bad, at Leastwise Not Dozier

Anything can happen now that everything has.

Don't you wish it is you who says that? I wish it is me who says that, only it is Dozier who says that. I cannot think of a single anything to say since writing this down is not my idea in the first place and is Dozier's idea, with Dozier saying to me, LaDonna darling, be my writing-down angel and write all this down like you are an angel come here to earth. Only some angel I am, not even knowing what to write down first. So I say to Dozier, What should I write down first? Only Dozier does not say anything, only is keeping his hands on the wheel and is keeping his eyes straight ahead on this road with the bugs shooting white out from the black from the both sides of this road like they are shooting at us. I wonder maybe Dozier is thinking about the same what I am thinking about and is not hearing me, only Dozier hears me all right, for after I watch the bugs shoot out some more and after I nearly quit thinking what I was thinking about that I told you about, and after I start getting asleepier and asleepier, which is the why this writing is slanting down now the way it is slanting down, Dozier says to me, LaDonna darling, write this, write anything can happen now that everything has. As you can see, I wrote that and also write what I just wrote.

This is maybe not what Dozier had in mind when he asked me to be his writing-down angel, only Dozier is the only this that I can think of right now to write down about. This is Dozier road-mapped out for you as Dozier is right now, starting with the nothing Dozier has on what he calls his mechanic tan southernmosts. Take Dozier's bare southernmost that is closest, the one on the gas, and jump your mind up halfway from the toe jam traffic jam to the top to the where there is squiggly green just under that what was Dozier's inside-all-day white skin as if somebody started squiggly drawing a road map down there using a green crayon to draw with. That little squiggle of green highway goes in under that white underside of ankle bone, then starts up again to spread out from that little higher-than-halfway-up muscle bunch of still down under Dozier. From that bunch of muscle-up, the in and out of green gets bigger, at leastwise looks bigger, gets to be what could be green interstates shooting up to the outside of what could be a side of the road rest stop on top of Dozier's old baldy worn bald by the rubbing of Dozier's blue jeans when Dozier is wearing blue jeans, only now Dozier is wearing baggy green Army cutoffs and a gray T. From under the sleeves of Dozier's gray T, the big seeable, what I call interstates, starts up again, bulk squiggling out again at the big humped-out muscle there that is half mechanic tanned and half sunburned red. Those interstates then squiggly dip down, then up, into the nearly all sunburned red before becoming four-lane divided dividing out into the underside of elbow to wrist before tunneling under, and here is the nearly, under the white under Dozier's watchband. The back of Dozier's sunburned hand, the one that is closest on the wheel, has the green forking out and running over itself into a kind of downtown busyness that ends with Dozier's fingernails rimmed in tarred parking lot black. Next comes Dozier's scenic overlook, starting with the sun-burned red yoking his neck and riding up to his clean-shaven unpaved that Dozier says he shaves every other day just for me. And there is Dozier's wooded parkland of curly black that if you were me you would not mind camping out in and maybe getting lost in. And talking about getting lost in, there is Dozier's toll limiteds that let me in in a way that I never wanted in before and do not want out of until what is the innermost of me is tongue driving around all the way down inside Dozier, driving down Dozier's throat and down inside and all around Dozier until looking out Dozier's eyes at what is the outermost of me writing this all down.

. . .

Already that everything that happened seems so long
ago, although in trying to figure back I guess it was only, if
today is already Friday, was only Tuesday, Wednesday, Thurs-
day, three days ago. Three days and another me, or so it seems
ago, when that me that is me now awoke up out of myself
asleep-walking through my life in a way that I did not even
know about until that everything that happened happened.
Maybe you know what I mean? Maybe something has happened to you to all of a sudden make you say to yourself,
Where have I been until now? How did I get anything done
until now? How did I get to where I am now? Three days and
a lifetime ago and here I am now with the heat rising wrinkly
off the road the way it is and whip shaking the hair on the off
sides of our heads the way it is and sucking in hot over us the
way it is and sticking us to these seats the way it is so that every
time one of us moves it sounds like somebody tearing tape.
Only all this wrinkly and all this whip-shaking straight and all
this sucking in hot and all this tearing tape of our skin means
that I am wide awake, at leastwise that I think that I am wide
awake, although the truth is it does seem a little like dreaming
with here we are where we are out here with Dozier riding us
to the anything that can happen next.

There is all that what Dozier is all about on the outside
that I road mapped out for you, then there is all that what
Dozier is all about on the inside. That all that what Dozier is
on the inside is not as easy to write down about as that what
is on the outside, not that that was that easy, only with me,
what you see, which is not all that much, is what you get. With
Dozier, what you see, at leastwise what you see on the outside,
seems a whole lot different than what is on the inside. On the
outside, Dozier looks like he can take care of himself and
anybody and anything else that needs taking care of. On the
inside, Dozier is . . . Dozier. What this girl is trying to say to
you the best I know how, which I know is none too good, is

that there inside of Dozier, in spite of what you might first think on first seeing Dozier, and in spite of what Dozier did or does, there is something that makes somebody like me want to do for Dozier the best I can. At the same time, there is also something else in me that wants to say that I most likely will never be able to do for Dozier, at leastwise not in the way that Dozier most wants, whatever that way is. Maybe that is true for all of us and those we love the most.

This is written down in the dark with Dozier having us settled in on sixty, only with this dark way out here the way it is, you, dear whoever you are reading this, will have to forgive me if this writing down is not all on the lines and is all over instead, only I have to write down to you now so that you should know to forget about most of the whatever you might hear about what Dozier and me did or did not do and about the everything that did or did not happen. The truth is, who other than Dozier and me and maybe Stepdaddy even really cares about the everything that happened? And the truth is that excepting for Stepdaddy's seventy-three-and-whatever-the-change-was, I bet, and maybe you can hear Dozier really doing the talking here and me trying to pass it off a little that it is me doing the talking here, only we bet that even Stepdaddy does not care all that much about what happened. Everybody we meet mostly seems to only care about and is only mostly talking about this weather, talking this sit-on-you heat and how there is no end to it in sight. Only to only tell you the truth some more, sometimes Dozier starts the weather talk himself by saying in his best-natured-Dozier way, Lots of weather we're having lately. Dozier says you can tell a lot about a person from whatever the way they answer that, if they even bother answering that. Knowing that, I say to you that whatever you most likely hear about Dozier and me and about what Dozier and me did or did not do and about the everything that did or did not happen is not worth knowing all that much about and just is.

. . .

Dozier says there is something about getting up early, about getting up either with first light or a little before so that you see the sun alight on the as-far-away-as-you-can-see. Dozier says there is something about that light and about that time of day that gives a someone a kind of hope, a kind of promise of what the day might bring. I say let me asleep, although that only time that I have gotten up that early, at leastwise after a while after that only time that I have gotten up that early, there was, and there still is, if I could only get up, all that not having to go anywhere we do not want to go, or do anything that we do not want to do, and that if we want we can spend all of the whole day out of this heat somewhere, stopping out at some spinachy sump hole somewhere out here to laze around in the back of the van and in the choked-off shallows talking about the all of what we want and what we will do and where we will go, or if we want we can just go, go five hundred miles north, south, east, west to see some of the nearly all of everything that I have never seen and most likely will never see again. And all that all, along with all of Dozier himself, is nearly enough to make me maybe think that Dozier is right about what Dozier says about getting up with that first light.

This is again maybe not what Dozier most likely had in mind for me to write down about when he asked me to be his writing-down angel, so this will be just between you and me, not that you might likely will want any of this anywhere near you once you know what this is. This can happen anywhere at anytime just like it just happened now with here we are with Dozier cruising Dozier and me who cares where with my hand cramping up with my writing all this down, when Dozier gets that little half look to himself like Dozier is amusing himself, not that there is anything so bad about amusing yourself, or even so bad about Dozier's little half look to himself so much as what comes after that look. What comes after that look is a kind of bark or a string of barks, and I do not mean a kind of bark the same as the bulldog's bark so much as a lower-kind-of-ripping-out-fast bark followed by Dozier saying, Uh-oh, trouser mice, or Uh-oh, listen to those trouser mice barking it up. And even Dozier's saying that is not so bad as what Dozier does next, especially in this all this heat sticking us to these seats as it is already and sweating us through what little we have on as it is already. And after Dozier does what he does, Dozier usually says something like, LaDonna darling, I know those trouser mice are loud, only don't you know the louder the better since the louder ones don't smell as bad as the softer ones smell. And when that does not work Dozier usually says something else like, LaDonna, between you and me darling, trouser mice between a man and a woman is the highest kind of closeness. And when that does not work either, Dozier usually says, LaDonna honey, do you think I would do this if I did not want to share with you the all of me there is to share, both the good and the bad that is the all of me? Only trouser mice are somehow not what I had in mind when Dozier so long ago already said to me, Well, are you coming? And here I am, trying to write all this all down the best I can and trying to love Dozier, the all of Dozier, the all of the good and the all of the bad of Dozier the best I can.

You are always in more shit than you think you are in. You can guess who it is who says that and you can also guess the other who it is who wishes she does not have to say that, only now does have to say that. You remember what I wrote you about hearing about what seemed like the everything that happened to Dozier and me that really did seem like everything, and in some ways was, only with nobody excepting Dozier and me and maybe Stepdaddy really caring? Only now there are some others who care about what happens and about what Dozier and me do or do not do. And I do not mean the same some others as maybe you who might have been wondering all along now how we have been getting along asleeping

and eating and all that. The answer to your wondering is that
we have been getting along better than all right, asleeping in
the back or on the roof of the van and eating wherever we can
find salad bars where you most likely already know that you
can fill up a tray with all the greens all glopped over with all
the chunked-up creamy that you could want. Anyway, to make
a short story shorter, seventy-three-and-whatever-the-change-
was, as much as that is, does not go as far as you might think,
even asleeping here in the van and eating all those glopped
over greens sometimes three times a day. And to tell you the
truth, even with our doing all that, I did not think all that much
about where the seventy-three-and-whatever-the-change-was
was going, even when we pull up way out here at one of these
self-serves. At this self-serve, there is this fat guy so fat that it
makes you wonder about laying off that all-over chunked-up
creamy, not that I have anything against fat guys or fat anyones
or fat anythings, at leastwise not that I know that I do, only this
fat guy is so fat sitting inside that little glassed-in and cinder-
blocked self-serve with all those ciggies and with all those
candy bars and with his little TV on and with his two little fans
blowing right on all his fat, that it just makes you wonder. Now
this fat guy, although I suppose it is not his fault that he is fat,
is so fat that even only just sitting there, just sitting and not
doing anything other than just sitting there, is still enough to
make his fat tremble around. So here we are and here is this
fat guy with his fat trembling around even more when this fat
guy, with his fat-guy hand and his fat-guy fingers, pushes out
the spring-loaded drawer at Dozier with Dozier putting in a
five and saying, Hidy, lots of weather we're having lately. And
this fat guy, with even his hair slicked straight back looking fat,
trembles around the lower half of his face with the word regular coming out. Dozier is not saying anything until I start
wondering maybe Dozier is not hearing the fat guy, only
Dozier is hearing the fat guy all right with Dozier saying, Regular, along with this lady, meaning me, would like to use your
dumper. And this fat guy, fat lips, fat chin, fat everything that

I can see gone all trembling around to fat says, There is a faucet out back. And Dozier says, This lady, still meaning me, don't need to use a faucet if you know what I mean. And the fat guy trembles back that the faucet out back is all there is to use. And Dozier says, Then what do YOU use when YOU have to use the dumper? Only before the fat guy can say something back for me to hear I am on my way out back to over near where the faucet is where nobody if they were around could really see me anyway, and squat down with my sun dress up in my arm crooks and watch the trickle thread itself out through the dust before skinning over to a stop. I try twisting the faucet on, only this faucet has not been used for a while, or if it has been used whoever used it last really twisted this faucet off tight so that even using both hands I cannot even start twisting this faucet on. I go back around to tell Dozier watching the PAY THIS AMOUNT rolling up, and tell him, when Dozier says all short, Here, you do this! So here I am doing the pumping with Dozier sticky popping over this hot sticky tar over to the glassed-in fat guy again when I notice that besides the sticky popping of Dozier's flip-flops, that Dozier has the bulldog stuck barrel down and mostly hanging out of the back pocket of Dozier's cutoffs, making Dozier's cutoffs droop way low down in back. The PAY THIS AMOUNT starts slowing down some with me clicking and squeezing out every last all what I can so that I only half hear Dozier say something to the cinder-blocked and glassed-in fat guy about how YOU, meaning the fat guy, really better take a look, when I half see the fat guy take his fat old time tremble heave himself off whatever he is sitting on and tremble huff himself the way really fat guys do over to the door and let himself out with a key and with the same key lock the door behind him when Dozier has the bulldog out. The fat guy, tremble huffing and rolling from side to side the way really fat guys do, looks back and sees Dozier has the bulldog out. I look around and see there is still nobody else around, just me and Dozier and the fat guy unlocking the door again, only this time to let in himself and Dozier. I clank up the nozzle seven cents over and twist on the cap and go around and get in. In that little glassed-over, and with the way Dozier and the fat guy seem to be moving so slow, they look to me as if they are moving underwater. Dozier and the fat guy look to me as if they are talking underwater with me not able to hear what they are talking about, only I bet it is not this weather, only then again with Dozier you never really know. They are talking with the fat guy doing most of the talking when Dozier, just as slow and as calm as Dozier can be, blaps the fat guy a slow one with the bulldog. Something black starts slow down the fat guy's no-longer-combed-straight-back fat-looking hair and the fat guy is doing something slow and underwater with his hands that I cannot see, while just as calm as can be, just as slow as can be, Dozier is slow stuffing with his hand which is not holding the bulldog something into the pockets of his green bagging-out cutoffs. Dozier stops his slow underwater stuffing, and just as easy going as Dozier gets, backs out the door. The hand not holding the bulldog is still in Dozier's pocket while the other hand is dangling, then pointing the bulldog down at the still-sitting-down fat guy. I can only say pointing even though I am seeing this all the while and not seeing or hearing the bulldog go off even once, never mind the twice the newspaper says, only I did see the fat guy all of a sudden look up at Dozier in a way that I knew that the fat guy all at once knew that whatever much shit he thought he was in before, that he was in a lot more shit now.

That feeling of having just awoke up out of myself that seems so long ago already, and is so long ago already, grows dreamier and dreamier with all this going and going and with all this fun-house-mirror-making-everything heat and with all this always-knowing heavy up inside me now that they, who-ever they are, are coming. Dozier says they are not the same they that I most likely think they are, and that they always come for you with smiles, and that they always come for you as friends, and that they always come for you at a time when you are at your weakest. Dozier says the only what we can do is keep doing what we are doing, keep going and going, keep trying to get around this heat, keep the bulldog wrapped up in the greasy rag right here on the seat between us, keep writing all this down to keep that feeling of having just awoke up out of ourselves from getting away from ourselves.

This is us, Dozier and me, and the more that is the us together and how most nights we try and get around this heat that is still lay-over-your-face hot. This is us, way away out here now with nothing other than a few jacks around and with nobody that we know of around and with nothing on, other than sweat, up on top of the van on top of Dozier's old asleeping bag. This is us, up here cooking in our own juices after making more than either of us alone could make. This is us, cooking and watching off at the thin wires of no noise lightning alighting up the clouds and the dark. From down in the dark below, Dozier has the game on with the talk of whoever that is talking now as almost close as somebody you have maybe known a long time, maybe an uncle on your momma's side that you love and that you maybe see once a year and has come to visit now and is in the room next to your room talking low. This is still us, still cooking through Dozier's old asleeping bag with all this all-over-us heat, only even with all our cooking through, only even with all the more that is the us together, there is still not enough us for me with me wanting and with me having Dozier's arm and Dozier's hand around and over and on me. This is me, tracing down from Dozier's snugged-down watchband without seeing anything about Dozier excepting the what that is Dozier that is in my head. This is me, blind tracing the hairs on the back of Dozier's hand to the bumped-up smooth of Dozier's crossing over and fanning out interstate offshoots that I now trace back the other way as far as I can trace back with the me inside my head wanting to be inside Dozier tracing all the way around the inside of Dozier until tracing, then finding, then staying forever safe right here in the heart of Dozier's heart.

Those they that are coming for us are here. Up here in these from-down-below-look-black-and-bleared-up hills are already cooler with the one way all the way up hairpinning around and up and around past the sliders, past the snow fields, until here we are, up here in the climbed-up-coolness with either the going all the way back down into that heat the same hairpinning way we came up, or the going on beyond through. Those they, and there are two of them, a him sitting there inside collecting, and a her standing there outside wearing a wide-brimmed and an open heavy the same as he is wearing, only her open heavy is humped up in back by a holstered with her looking in and nodding in and saying something in to the each of the three ahead, then two, then here we go with the wrapped-up bulldog on the seat between us and with her nodding in and looking in at Dozier with Dozier saying, Lots of weather we're having lately, and her not saying anything, only looking in at Dozier with her face having lost all the how do. Dozier's face has that half look like he is amusing himself that stays that way until her finally saying, Enough weather to suit me, with Dozier holding out the five and the two ones and her saying to Dozier, Hand it to him, and Dozier pulling up and handing him the five and the two ones and me looking and finding one quarter, then another quarter to make the fifty, and me handing the fifty to Dozier with Dozier handing the fifty to him with him saying, Thank you, and with Dozier not saying anything more, only going and going until they are way back there and we are gone.

Dozier and me are fat wrapped in the all that we have to put on against this way-the-way-up-here-watch-yourself-smoke-out-the-inside-of-yourself. Dozier is still asleeping down in that tunneled-down warmth that was us caterpillered together down inside in the barely-able-to-breathe that is Dozier's old asleeping bag. That was us that is, until me awaking up and wriggling up and unzipping and rolling out and zipping Dozier back up. The moon making was ghosting down enough for me to see by to get out this notepad and to open to this page only without me writing anything down to you without first watching the soft asleeping little hills that was and is Dozier still asleeping, then watching all the what I can watch from up here on top of the van of the black flatness that is the lake, of the higher-up moon-blue belt that is snow, of the rounded straight-up black of these surrounding hills that I watch until nearly all the skim-milky ghosting down has all but ghosted away leaving the rounded animal backs of these hills rimmed with day. That is when I start slow writing this what I just wrote down to you with me knowing what you are most likely thinking about now and have most likely been thinking about for a long time before now. I say to you do not worry the way I am no longer worried for I know that no matter what happens from here on in that at leastwise Dozier has already been delivered and saved, if only because I have been Dozier's writing-down angel. **Q**

die

He often dreamed of a hero's death

Icarus

The fall? I don't even remember it.
I blacked out halfway down, the ocean spinning
in wide circles with the coast, green and
brown blurring together—I didn't see much else.
Now you tell me I'm a symbol: impetuous youth,
the dangers of adolescence, even suffering that
nobody notices except painters and poets.
You've got to admit it's all pretty
hard to believe—like I was a special case or
something. Think about all those kids Minotaur
had for dinner; nobody made a big deal about
        them.
They just went crawling down into the dark
in their clean white robes and became statistics.
I mean, it makes you wonder, the kind of things
people decide to remember. It's like
all the inventions my old man has a patent on:
sails, axes, saws, even glue; and what do they
make a fuss over but a sex toy he carved
for old Minos's wife and a drafty maze
to house her monster—and, yeah, I almost
forgot, a pair of defective wings.

GEORGE FRANKLIN

Jeanne Duval

Elle ignore l'Enfer comme le Purgatoire,
Et quand l'heure viendra d'entrer dan la Nuit noire,
Elle regardera la face de la Mort,
Ainsi qu'un nouveau-né,—sans haine et sans remord.
—BAUDELAIRE

Of course I was unfaithful, but
what a funny word that is—as though
faith had anything to do with it.
He was the kind, understand, who likes
to watch as much as do, and imagine
even more than watch. There are quite
a few of those down here. If this
wind lets up, I'll show you some. That's
why I was amused so by your phrase.
You see, the more I was "unfaithful,"
the better he liked it, though I
don't think he'd confess that even now.
Look how he glares at me with those
big eyes of his, sunken and dark.
There was a dog once in our quarter
who had eyes like that. Each morning
he'd drag himself along the quay, always
hoping someone would drop a rind of
moldy cheese or a stale piece of bread.
I suppose he finally starved, because
after a while we didn't see him anymore.
He was such a useless creature; no one
in his right mind would take him in.
But I don't want to bore you with
things like that, especially since
you've traveled such a distance just to talk

with us. Perhaps you'd like to know how it was
we met. I was an actress then, and not in
the provinces either. I forget which play it was,
but afterwards, a photographer,
a friend of his, introduced us. I thought
he had a lot of money the way he spent:
dresses, jewels—and poems too. You
may have seen those. They sounded quite
impressive when he read them, though
I don't pretend to be any sort of judge.
At first, I think it was my hair
appealed to him, ebony black and scented,
a thick chignon that hung against
my neck. (These winds, you know, are worse
than tropics for the hair.) Anyway,
he called me his "marmoset" and his "sultana,"
and I'd pose for him across my bed
with only a necklace on and some bangles.
It wasn't until his cash ran out that
I became "leech" and "vampire." That was
vicious of him. Already I was more
his nurse than lover. Oh, he'd caught
the disease years before we met and never
said where he got it or from whom.
Did I love him? That's a peculiar
question. I can't say I've ever thought
about it much, though I stayed with
him long after anyone could think
he was a bargain. Yes, I suppose you
could say I loved him. After all,
I wouldn't be here if I hadn't.

In the Service of Others

Those who waved goodbye had reasons
for not using their hands,

those malformed flowers that resembled
too many others, even the well-tended.

When we failed to come back
or came back not entirely ourselves

they wrung those hands. Indifference
had made them all but useless.

One woman with a reputation
for remembering used her body to reach me

and from that good night on could not
understand why she went to bed late,

then later, until not sleeping at all.
Her stare became her story. Friends

not knowing whom to blame, blamed themselves.
They spoke of anger as a jack-in-the-box

and sent toys they had bought on sale.
They were the good friends who understood

these things, who threw themselves,
instead of flowers, to the wind.

Reverie

I am not your wife now
anymore than I ever was.
On the gray sand by a green sea

if I had not overheard people talking
about the distribution of happiness,
I would have felt invisible, like

a woman hearing voices or the voice
of one child in the distance,
or a husband's, beside her.

Not the water, the gulls whirling
wind-tacked, but the sound
of your breath overlapping mine

is what I hear. At night, should I hate
you for that, or myself for dreaming?
Tonight I will knock on your door and ask

to be let in. I will be like parchment
to a scholar, dirt to a saint.

The Stars of Grand Central

I wonder if you know the stars
in the ceiling of Grand Central,
if you've seen those pistolcracks of light
from withering bulbs set in a blue
you've never seen at night. And all around,
the constellations in gold paint:
Orion shows off his new buckle
while the bull dips his horns,
the twins argue over some possession
as the crab tiptoes away,
the fish look old and tossed,
as though the sky were a shelf of oxygen,
and the water-bearer pours and pours,
water hitting rock with the sound
of a thousand feet across a marble floor.

Tell me which of these proves
the God who is or is not there:

[1]

A man in a suit is walking to the Grand Central
        subway,
and he stumbles. His briefcase falls,
cracks open, tosses papers in a chirpy skid
like small friction toys all across the floor.
They are lost beneath feet hurrying home;
anyone can see it, they are lost
and deserve to be forgotten,
but the man in the suit falls to his knees
and begins a crawling collection,
bumped by knees, tripped over, cursed, until,

looking like a father about to give a piggyback ride,
he drops his head and carefully
begins to weep.

[2]

A man without arms sits propped
against the building. It is spring.
He is drunk, and his happy breath blooms in the
    air.
Beside him a tubercular Vietnamese woman
squats and pours vodka into his mouth.
They are dying and they don't care.
Still, this is killing him.
Still, she fills his throat like a goblet.
Still, he drinks until the overflow
pops from his mouth and dives
like the best kid you ever saw
right into his shirt.

From these proofs we can determine
we become what we craft,
and what we have made
is the stars of Grand Central, which,
unnoticed and silly,
remain all night to guide travelers who are not lost,
the bulbs burning out one by one,
the blue ceiling ever darkening,
the golden figures falling upward,
falling from substance into what was never made,
thinking the jangle in our pockets
is the clash of ten thousand thousand suns.

The Sleepless Man in the Pony Nation

He mends by moonlight in an old rocking chair.
White ponies canter across the backs of his hands.
He wears his face like a hat with black feathers.
How can a night fill his throat and speak not a
      word?

His life is a big decision that does not matter.
It is like a dirt road blown for centuries
by countless winds, yet in the same place every day.

He loves the ponies kicking through their gray
      grasses.
Love surges in a panic, the night in the throat,
he cannot help it, he loves it all
even though or because it will always run away.

The Mud Horse

The rain can turn me around,
make me see, for example, the woman
caught in it without protection,
her hair holding her face close,
and atop her collarbone,
drops caught in briefest sunlight,
preparing to leave, a necklace of water,
and I am gone, in love yet again.
At times like these
it seems dying has nothing to offer.

The TV news is farther north, in Petaluma,
where a foaling mare, buried five days
in a mudslide, has been found alive.
Every six and every eleven,
further developments on the Miracle Mud Horse,
taking small nourishments, lying on a waterbed,
learning to stand again,
its hooves amazed by unmoving ground.

It seems every wreckage provides
one such survivor, the baby surrounded
by the congress of the dead,
and always the rescuer who says,
We almost missed her.
We walked right by, and then we heard
a kind of whimpering, like an animal.
The Miracle Baby,
every six, every eleven,
the edifice of hope
where the angels imagine we live.

But the dead cannot forget us.
They do not know why their bodies must burn
to give us sustenance,
why the wind between their ribs
smells so sweet to us still living,
we, the miracle babies,
leading to everlasting pastures our mud horses.

This winter the wind bows the bridges,
and cats look out at the rain
from under my house, conversing all night
in twangy accents of complaint,
and trees are shoved aside
like old men on a sidewalk.
The mud horses settle along hillsides to foal,
no stars, the dirt pregnant too,
tenderly watching the grunting shapes,
preparing to fill the nostrils and mouths
of the newly born, to assume the form,
for our sakes, of the mares,
giving us in its kindness,
for a future we can finally love,
mud horses to carry us,
blindfolded, to the banquet.

Cellar

This is where we keep them: toy trucks
With busted wheels, the broken stuff
We can't get rid of, our old books,
The splintered chair, the fractured tabouret.

There's something stagey in our garbage.
The furniture is theatrical and grim.
Our repudiated gestures still live there,
Six feet under the kitchen. They wear
The vague insulted look of slighted relatives,
Belonging, but pushed aside.
                                    The dark place gives
Reluctant nobility to these disowned things.
I picture other broken objects down here,
Not always on view: behind the dead palm,
A litter of stillborn phrases, the snapped
Bunches of words, the shivered promises,
Those dusty entreaties that still snatch the throat—

Importunate as panhandlers or evangelists,
Those smirking beggars around Christmastime
Whose shrill, patched clothes shine in the snowy
     light.

Taxes

We've been here
for two years
with the woman officially
slumped over
                    falling out
of her bra
polka-dot stockings
and lack of exercise
                    except for tabulation
lost in poems
waiting
waiting and cracking
jokes with the growing pool
of patients
discuss last night's heavyweight fight
in the paperwork
he sweats through gains and losses
losing it
            over my head
sinking under.

What Happened to My Mother

Your clarity was a razor
       at my throat
when I was too young
     to judge,
and I've been chasing
  today
     ever since.

We were strangers
    before I understood
that old nightmares
   are only excuses
    not to love
what lies beyond
   our persuasion.

Now my heart stutters
  at your disguises
as you come and go
   like a summer shower.

We've become portraits
     of our battles,
you locked within arthritic bones,
me numb with burns.

Each day we struggle
    to become visible,
until the light
  dodges us into exhaustion,
  or we catch fire.

Prisoner

No fog horn
            moans
    when the glass
        we dream through
    breaks
            into a mist
    inhaled with every breath.

So much never changes
        or predictably recurs
    that we think
        we're still dreaming
and the straitjacket
    slipped around us
            feels like the wind
            instead of
    someone else's nightmare.

JOHN DE STEFANO

Poem

This is the prompt science.
This is the antic sorrow.
This begins: O, exact,
exaggerates, and ends
in ellipsis. It is
not the opposite of life.

Woman without likeness,
you have never been famous
for delivering on schedule.
What discipline in desire
that makes us over
and over forgive
the same mistake?

Dead Christ

From the slab walls of museums they rise,
    the flat, glassed
gods of the Quattrocento,
        the muscle
of the Renaissance emerging slowly,
painters finally seeing
how even flesh could be used. Their canvases
    answer
the faces of tourists
with the stunned faces of saints,
        the Virgin
sucked up to heaven in her blue robes. Or Adam
and Eve hung sorrowing, eye level,
          mirrors
of the drab and secret places of the soul.

Michelangelo painted the eternal father,
old and gray,
      like Zeus,
leaning forward, almost angry,
finally unable to stand his solitude.
Titian's Christ
rejects the touch of the world
    with infinite tenderness.

I claim only
the dead Christ of Mantegna,
the body simple as a house broken into,
    its scarred
borders relaxed of their power.
The unbleeding stigmata trace

precise circles on the hands,
the feet,
       the feet
looming in the forefront pleading
for the uselessness of the body. Lips pressed
in a tired line. The ribs timbered and delicate
on the arc of the chest. One old, sorrowing
   woman's
profile pushed into the frame,
her hooked nose and cheeks withered into half
   moons
     suggesting
how circular the grief they pass
       is, how it is both
   entrance and exit, salt
and wound.

In Fruit

Whether it was his mouth yearning
for that ripeness,
or my mouth, it felt like hunger.
Back then, the dogwoods spread like hills.
Their flowers had nothing
to mourn, flawless
as the first soul. Each tree
thicker than a man at the trunk, so that Joseph,
lying in the shade, grew small. Root
or tendril, his life suddenly a limb
of that force.
                    Cherry trees
pink with spring as gauzed blood—
And I saw it, that one fruit, ripe
though the tree was still in bloom and bees
droned seed into its flowers; a single
cherry, nestled with the blossoms
the way an idiot nestles
with the very young.
                         I felt it then,
strong, so strong, but not mine—
appetite without need. Joseph, angry,
avoiding my eyes, refused to pluck it.
Remembering the cries, the breath
of *whore* added to the wind's breath
in the marketplace . . . The fruit
offered itself, rich as wine, and my hand
rose . . . It burst
in my mouth, answer
to a question not mine, and I felt
that sudden life, like water on my tongue.

Supplication to the Photograph of Emiliano Zapata, and Praise

Help me, Emiliano, *hermano.*
My wings gone, I have only
my arms now, to lift me,
to thicken the air
with remembered flight.
Madre Dios!
My shoulder blades hurt
like hell. *Si,* I've given up
my dream of wax.

By the way, I must say,
you look dashing, wreathed
in this year's Palm Sunday palms.
Claro, hombre, I kept my promise:
went right up to the altar
after Mass and took them.

Three Headless Goddesses, One Sitting Apart:
Parthenon, East Pediment

There is always one like Hestia, staring
into distance when the other girls
are dancing together the quick thrusts
of the tango or practicing the dip,
their twelve-year-old hair brushing the floor,
tits spilling from Dacron blouses.
They practice kisses, their little-girl
tongues in each other's mouths.
Practice makes perfect, and perfect
is what they'll give the boys next
weekend, slippery as conches, their nipples
nacrosed, shining. Yes, there is always
a Hestia looking away when the other
girls massage each other,
making sure the boys are watching
as they lean back in each other's laps,
like this grown-up goddess with her mother,
Aphrodite and Dione, sharing the ease
of old lovers, Aphrodite's elbow
spreading her mother's thighs. She is making
herself comfy in the other's woman's groin,
the two of them at the movies, a man's
arm accidentally slipping as he pops
open the popcorn container. Even
mother-daughter love is more
than Hestia can bear, a mother's
tit sheer embarrassment,
too much like a cock, and something runs
from both, milky, the baby's face
turning itself inside-out
with desire, the nipple

so frantic it's already
unzipped, jerking off on air.
Who needs heads when these two
could find each other in the dark,
Aphrodite's garments flowing
in and out of her mother's, the merest
murmuring, barely audible. The virgin
goddess can neither understand it
nor fully shut it out.

Pornography

This panel of writers sits smoking. They're French.
Weathered faces reflecting the tough job
of figuring out life.
The exception is dressed in black, wearing shades,
a shank of blonde braid over her shoulder.
She's bored. New York bores her.
Bored, her red lips work carefully
sifting the air
of the stagnant auditorium.
    On the influence of World War II?
No influence, she says. It's dull. Dull and stupid.

I imagine her as a Vichy collaborationist. That
    striking poise
as the champagne glasses clink
from a distant explosion.
Her elegant cardinal gown
down in one smooth pulse,
Assistant Minister of Propaganda
grinning.
    A droning clock,
heavy breasts relaxing
as her secretarial fingers unwork the stiff buttons
on her khaki blouse. Yes, she's a Nazi.
A Nazi with fishnet stockings and legs to the moon.
The tall incredible arrogance of her.

I catch just a glimpse, memory of a bus
hurtling through the regal tapestry of night just
    west of Needles

and the Arizona border. Corrugated rubber mats
    littered
with aqua Filet O' Fish containers, flattened fries,
    husks of wrapper.
And I remember the stolen magazine with three
    women high
on stiletto heels, clutching impotent riding crops,
accepting with mellifluous mute sighs
the Nazi generals. Bending
to the joy of authority. Giving it
with a private smile.
Laws turned in upon themselves,
animate in the hollow place
of fantasy.

And I remember liking it.

Souls in Purgatory

I hadn't quite realized I had died
before the man in the plaid pants came in
to ask the way to the bathroom and we went
together down an alley in the old neighborhood

where little Mrs. Ferris was holding up
her lost cat's collar and she said You sons
of bitches put this pussy in the sky
I know you did, and I said this was true

while Al over here was numb with glee to think
it could have meant that much at all
to two such desperadoes as the likes of us
if they had Pussy in Paradise.

By My Lights

[I]

Used to be the sun was our only source of light,
not counting God, of course.
Then came fire,
a good thing for keeping a little of the dark
and marauding beasts at bay,
and for sitting around telling tales,
and for keeping warm,
and for making the meat tender and succulent.
Fire was good, too, because its radiant leaping
made your shadow leap.

[II]

The sunlight that falls through my window
can't lift itself off the floor
but has to crawl over to the wall
to prop itself up.
Eight fluorescent ceiling lights scatter
my shadow eight times around the room.
So long as I stay still,
those shadows will lie there quietly
until I move
or someone throws the switch.

If the Inquisition Had Come to Coffee

The coffee was safe in its shaded cups, the grapes
on the plate were smug in their cloudy skins
when the evening sun like an iron bar
levered open the end of the porch
and hung its ruddy beacon where we sat.

With this new light behind you, every word you
    spoke,
every gesture you made showered sparks
like meteors entering the atmosphere, and I saw
that your head was a planet in her quarter phase
and the moth circling your face was a moon.

If the inquisitorial magistrates had been there to
    see you
as I saw you then, I think the true relation of sun
to earth and stars might have been revealed to
    them,
and Galileo with his telescope and Jupiter and the
    mountains
of the moon could with ease have balanced for the
    rest of us
the forces of faith and reason in one peaceful orbit.

Counting the Colors of Sycamores

The colors of most trees are two,
leaf and bark,
as one can see in any kindergarten crayon,
or three if we add autumn,
rough and empty being not colors,
as is popularly supposed,
but rather absence of leaf
or perhaps qualities of winter space
as when unplaned planks of light
slant through the upper limbs of elms.

But the colors of the blessed sycamore
are five, not counting leaf and bark,
and all five reward precise enumeration:

First is splendor,
   spans of forty-pointed leaves adorn
   the pallid footpaths of the moon;

Second, sprinkle,
   as when ropes of blackbirds chuckle
   through its bony tangles;

Third comes grace,
   a glaze on wind-clad branches
   in their upward dance;

Fourth, there's shadow,
   as when starlight dusts
   its limbs with silence;

Fifth is death,
        that smooth and brittle face
        of possums grinning at the dark.

The Owl Counts Four

Mourning from
the sycamore
at my back door,
the owl counts four,
father, mother,
me, and one more.

Recuperating Leslie

The great man's wife is anxiously walking
The length of the old-fashioned swimming pool
Deep in their deep green yard
On a sweltering July day in Buffalo.
She is keeping a close eye on him because
If she averts her eye for even an instant,
A stream of blood may gush out of his nether
    regions,
Staining the pale water he placidly pushes aside
As he makes his stately way
Up and down the pool as specified.
Her gaze is keeping him alive.

He is recovering well, she says.
It was a close call, she says.
He has never spent the night in a hospital
Before, not even to be born, she says,
And he just turned seventy, so you could say
It will be good practice for the future.

They have run out of Jell-O Pops,
But a colleague has rushed
To the store to fetch more
And the egg salad sandwich
Waits in the fridge
With the cranberry juice and the cantaloupe cubes.
This is the soft diet his M.D. prescribed.

Recuperating Leslie gives three cheers
For remedies with his soft wife
On a soft afternoon

While he plies the soft waters
Before emerging like a shaggy manatee,
To shake, to dry his soft gray hair
And bask in old affection
Back in the softness of his summer chair.

The Hang-Glider

FROM AN ALBUM, INCOMPLETE

Here's the earliest, black and white.
You bend over your small son and your wife
Smiles straight out at me.

At the airport we strike a formal pose,
Your arm around my shoulder like an owner.
I'm in my same old departure dress.

I ask you for a picture by the pond.
Lazy, sated, sun in your face,
You sprawl, a big lug.

But back on the tractor, masterful,
You and the ancient machine engage
In slaughter with the underbrush.

Or stalking the high night meadow
Under the moon, an orange paste-up,
You find a new view for ploughing.

Sometimes, playing Icarus,
You sail from sand dunes over the ocean,
Grinning under gold and purple wings.

When you test stiff winds,
Flouting the mist,
I think I'll never see you again.

CAPE KIAWANDA, AT THE COAST

Often in late September light
You clambered hand over hand
Up the steep bluff

Lured by the urgent promise of the sky.
And it was like wings!
Brave painted silk all bold

And purple in the cold autumn air.
Stripes flapped you into action,
The glider struggling to launch itself

Out over sullen water.
What to do, after all,
With so much sky and water

But to pitch out & up & over
And try, with wild extravagance, to fly?
Then the bright wings failed.

At dusk, on a cliff by the Pacific,
You fell, face-down into colors
Crumpled like the strings of silk

Magicians pluck from their sleeves.
And died, amazed,
While strangers pounded your chest

And a clumsy truck lurched down the beach
To fetch your sweet body back
And burn you into ashes.

for Anthony Ostroff

Star-Gazing in the City

Not a serene habit but intermittent,
I rode the curved tracks of a black vault
to the end.

Not a place to entrust oneself to darkness,
I came out to night,
to an agitated crowd

pointing up at the madman in his window
who, like some stars, never looked down,
who, as an unknown star,

had surfaced uncertainly
from the curtained depths.
In relief, remote

from our revolution below,
he rode the curved track of his flight
to the end.

The demented woman
pulled at her hair
incessantly
and kept calling
him Ob'jay

Most tadpoles don't make it to even Frogdom. They get eaten from above and below. Down from up in sky, blue herons eat them up; up from under mud of pond, lungfish eat them up. Tadpole calls me other day from way out west on crazy coast. "In hospital again," he tells me. I say, "No, why? You're okay. Only have that ARC thing." Sounds good, like Noah's boat, saves what's left of world, two by two. ARC means only have a little bit of germ. "My blood's not clotting," Tadpole says. I say, "So what? Does mine?" Pinch myself to see. Clot, those things I bleed, losing babies on the way. "Means won't stop," he says. I say, "Oh, no! That's a thing for kings and queens." Read that book, don't marry your cousins. Who wants to? Used to try to drown mine. Buried cousin, Jerry Jim, up to his neck in dirt till Aunt Rita stopped me. "I am a queen," Tadpole laughs, his not-really laugh. "Tomorrow they want to take my spleen," he says. I ask, "What's a spleen? Keep it, please. Ask other doctors. Get three opinions." Tadpole pauses, hear tears in his voice, "Why? Be three times as confused and nobody knows." Getting boring, Tadpole's dying, keeps taking me with him, off and on, for three years now, via telephone. All movies end. Books, too, most not soon enough. Only this day, only this day lasts forever. But Tadpole is young, only twenty-three, not like me, having made it long time now in Frogdom. When first we met in western desert like Holy Land, at Round-up Ranch, the rich man's manager, Tadpole was hard on cocaine trail, had been out five years, lovers everywhere and all their seed to drink. We went drinking, you and I, up the mountains and into the cowboy bars. You liked cowboys. Tadpole wants to go to Europe with me. Hang around cafés on Left Bank. Get our usual A in café. Wrote song, "I get an A in café/That's where I spend my whole

day/Other students came to work/But I came to play/I get an
A in café." Went to Louvre once. Mona Lisa, dusty, tired-
looking. Think of old stripper once knew named Original
Mona Lisa. Liked her better than painting. That summer Tadpole got sick, went in hospital, so I went to Paris for both of
us, picked up strangers all cross-continent like we always do.
While I play in Paris all summer long, Tadpole, in hospital, is
injected with live penicillin, then steriods. Medicine made him
sicker. Writes me letter, sends to Paris. Spleen in little dictionary: ductless organ near stomach. Get big dictionary: visceral
organ composed of white pulp and red pulp. Did you ever see
a lassie go this way and that way and this way and that way and
this way and that way? Why am I so afraid? What did we do?
Any of us? All of us? Tadpole banged hundreds of boys and
some are wrong and Eliot is wrong, this is the way the world
ends, with a bang. Even Tadpole eggs fed things, made circle
go. I'm an old toad growing a wart. Tadpole wants to come to
Chicago or wants me to come to California, I know why, to say
goodbye, but I want to go to Paris again or maybe Rome will
feel like home. I never say goodbye, Tadpole, I slink away.
Right now I'm slinking with my new friend, Yeats. So let the
rain fall down, let the rain fall down, who gives a damn! Do you
remember, remember everyone, everybody, at ranch cried
when we left? People never want you to go home, leave the
party, and we never disappoint them. Until now, that is. **Q**

I am busy ripping my hands to meat in my once-a-day, everyday, fight-to-the-death-or-die rodeo wrestle-off that I am only too happy to have with that evil-hearted, son-of-a-bitch of a circular saw blade that the checkout girls up front call the bane of my meatful existence and which I do not call much of anything except a pain in my meat-cleaning ass, with the radio going louder than they let me on nothing at all but the AM meat-cutter's Muzak anything-but-rock-and-roll, freezer-box, cleaver-headed, don't-you-touch-that-dial-Mr.-Meat-Room-Cleaner-Upper that they never let me change, just to keep any random so-called thoughts I might be lucky enough to have from spilling out of my head down here, when this guy Steve sticks his big mint-face-deuce-patty of a mug in the display case and starts poking finger holes in the plastic wrapping on the packages of what we at Super Duper are calling this week's ground-chuck special.

Steve is a dude I sort of know from this math class we are in called Problems and Statistics, and he is always busting my chops on how all the dudes we know are either one or the other or on their way to becoming both. But I have seen Steve chug down a big twelve-ouncer of what he calls the dreaded green death in nothing flat when his rents let him trash their house on weekends, and I have watched Steve suck the fire out of a full-packed bong and hold it in for what he calls the evil TI before the flame hits his thumb on the match, so I figure I can deal with Steve and his finger-poking escapades better than most of the drens they call people in this place we call a town.

Besides which, I am too hip-hop hipping as Grand Master of the meat, the beatest meat-cleaner of them all in what the checkout girls up front call my pepperoni purgatory to bother with the dick-head customers out there who seem to get their jollies out of diddling with the plastic wrapping on the packages of this week's ground-chuck special—especially when I've got that snaggle-toothed tiger of a circular saw blade wriggling like a string of chain-linked sausages in what I used to call my hands, but which are getting so T-bone red and raw that I sometimes think I am next in line for what the checkout girls up front call the Spaz-of-the-Week-Award that they said they wanted to give to Eddy, the bug-eyed, pork-brained meat cutter who thinks he is my boss and who tells me things about the Board of Health and all of what he calls the pain and suffering I will bring to the meat eaters of this town if I do not clean that circular saw blade to perfection every single day, because the checkout girls up front say Eddy's hands are so weirded-out by now that he does not have a lifeline anymore.

> *Warning! Exercise caution while using this machine. Rotating parts inside.*

I watch Steve pick up a package of this week's ground-chuck special and weigh it in his hands. It looks to me as if Steve is waiting for me to say something, but I cannot tell what it is. Then all at once, as if we'd been rapping to it, Steve says, Did you ever notice how people never change? And he flips the package of this week's ground-chuck special end over ground-chuck end in a big, slow, red-and-white cleaner-hating arc that goes from display case to meat room floor, where it lands face down in a puddle of blood and meat and where it will stay until the checkout girls up front are gone and no one else is here and I can stash it back in the display case and make like nothing ever happened.

They just get more like themselves, Steve says. I try to think about what Steve means when he raps like this, or if there is something more I should be doing, but before I can start to crank up a little of what Steve calls periodic mental activation, the circular saw blade snaps out of my hands and into the air where Steve and I can watch it spin around a while before it lands at my meat-cleaning feet in a tinny, circular-saw-blade kind of way that makes me want to crash out in the freezer and start hurting things again.

Do not operate while under the influence of alcohol or drugs. Do not put hands in chopper.

There's a FEE tomorrow, Steve says, and I think he means a test in Prob and Stat. Steve has been trying to get everyone in class to say FEE, for Friendly Educational Experience, and I think I am supposed to say something, or do something with my hands, whenever Steve says FEE, but I do not know what it is. I try to think of something I can do to show Steve I still have what he calls a clue in life, but nothing good comes out, so I stand there in what the checkout girls up front call all my meat-room glory and wait for Steve to fill me in on this business with the FEE.

But all Steve says is, TEE City, dude. And this time I think he is saying TEE, for Tragically Educational Experience, which is what Steve says your life will be if you forget about a FEE and what most of my tests are, anyway.

I hear the radio start calling itself the only source of news I can use, so I go to turn it down. I watch Steve do a kind of one-armed handstand over the display case and think about what it must be like not to have to work all day and how nice it would be if I could just be Steve for a while. Then Steve says, Tell me who I am. I watch him close his eyes and stand still, with his hands at his sides. He twitches his upper lip a few times and says something like Blue, Blue, Priscilla Blue. Then Steve opens his eyes and looks at me. Elvis Presley, he says, and he laughs a little bit. Then Steve stands that way again, with his eyes closed, except that this time he taps on the back of his head and makes some kind of blowing-up sounds with his mouth. John F. Kennedy, Steve says. And I see Steve is doing his imitations of famous people who are dead.

Massive kegger, Steve says when he is through doing John F. Kennedy, BTOBS. And I think this is Steve's way of saying Be There Or Be Square. Then I watch Steve turn around and take what the checkout girls up front call his perma-buzzed brain waves up the frozen-food aisle to the front of the store, where I suppose he will try to score some heavy-duty convo action and narc on the bogus-head meat cleaner down here who forgot about the FEE and who loves his job so much that he will never ever leave.

Disconnect power while cleaning this machine.
Failure to do so could result in severe electric shock.

When Steve is far enough away so I do not see him anymore, I turn up the radio and try to snag a little of what Steve calls the only source of news you can lose. I pick up the circular saw blade and groan my daily meat-room groan and think about the kegger coming up on Friday night. And in the background, just below my random so-called thoughts, I hear the radio start to say something about charred remains. And gasoline. And what it calls suicide on a quiet, tree-lined street. I listen some more and I think, maybe Steve should hear this stuff, so I move over to where I can see him better and yell for him to check it out.

And then I hear the name.

I look back out into the store called Super Duper and see that Steve is messing with some boxes in the frozen-food aisle. I do not think he has heard me, so I turn the radio down and go back to cleaning the circular saw blade. I wipe off the bits of meat and bone with my meat-room cleaning rag and I think, Go away, Steve. Go. I watch Steve standing in the frozen-food aisle and I try to push him out of the store with my thoughts. After almost never leaving, Steve looks as if he might be leaving Super Duper. I watch him step in front of what the checkout girls up front call the Star Trek doors, and then Steve disappears, probably on his way over to the CVS drug store, where he can scarf some crunch off the candy girls and generally make a geek of himself trying to get them to crash what he still must think will be a massive kegger at his house on Friday night.

And then I guess Steve will head on back to what the radio calls the quiet, tree-lined street. Later on the checkout girls up front will turn out all the lights and leave me here alone, with the radio going louder than they let me on you-know-what and the evil-hearted circular saw blade ripping up my hands and my thoughts of Steve and what he will find when he gets to the place he used to call his home.

And then it will be tomorrow, and we will all be back here at Super Duper. And I will have to wrestle with the circular saw blade all over again, and Eddy, the bug-eyed, pork-brained meat cutter who thinks he is my boss will be hassling me for whatever his meat-cutter's brain can come up with to hassle me about, and maybe we will talk about it and maybe we will not. Maybe there will be jokes to tell about flame-broiled mothers. Or how Mrs. Steve's Mom will be on special next week at such and such a pound. But mostly I don't think any of us will really know what to do or think or say. And that is when I think we will all just try to keep on going, with what everyone here calls our Super Duper life, as if nothing bad or evil ever thought to come our way.

> *Warning!*
> *Circular saw blade must be cleaned after every use*
> *by order of the Board of Health.*
> *Violators will be prosecuted to the full extent of the law.* **Q**

SAINT FRANCIS FEEDS RAISINETS TO THE TEENAGERS OF ASSISI

circa 1220

O'Donnell

ETERNAL ICE-CREAM

at the grave of the inventor of frozen food

ATTILA THE HUN
REBORN IN A RABBIT'S BODY
perforce harmless — Belgium, 1951

O'Donnell

GOD CREATING AN OBSCENE ANIMAL

"No, no- you want Hamlet, Prince of <u>Sweden</u>."

But in the morning, will I still be your best friend?

APPLIANCE DAY AT LOURDES

A FROG THAT LOOKED VERY MUCH BUT NOT CONFUSINGLY LIKE A WOMAN

Its small size gave it away.

(Bath, England, 1932)

O'Donnell

Episode #4

This forest fire was splendid, it was prodigal, Fire #33 burning up 3,456 acres or something like that. They took me up in a two-passenger helicopter. My partner The Shooter says helicopters have a godlike aspect in that they levitate and ascend vertically when they leave the earth and also that they throw up such a roar and an amount of debris that people bend down and avert their faces. There were three, four big ones levitating and ascending from the fire base. They were bucket-bombing the hot spots. The pilot took off the door so I could hang out and shoot pictures, and I saw what an appreciable amount of air was between me and the ground. The pilot doesn't give a shit if you fall out. He just wants to whizz us around the fire and then get back to bucket-bombing. I don't think they're into flying picture-taking people around. We were about two hundred feet over this enormous spruce that torched; that's what the fire fighters say. They say "torch." It was on the edge of the hottest part of the burn and I guess it was surrounded by so much pure-D temperature that it went incandescent in seconds. The fire shot up it and it burst, it started burning sideways, like an explosion. You can't imagine hanging over this kind of thing, hovering and levitating, as it happens. We had headsets with mikes so everybody could talk to each other because the chopper is making these movie sound-track chopper sounds. I heard the pilot say, "God, I can't wait to get rid of these shooters and get back to bucket-bombing." Then we landed in some muskeg because I wanted a shot of the ground crew and they did it, they all fell to their knees in attitudes of devotion and put their hard hats over their faces as we came down. That's the other thing; because of the rotor-drop, you have to grovel and sort of crawl up to the helicopter when you board it, and do the same thing in reverse as you leave The Presence. The really big ones come down among the crews at the fire base and there are all these groveling fire fighters with chips and shit and dust and bits of gravel flying. These guys go at fire fighting as if it were a military operation. They speak of the "initial attack" and fires that "resist attack." Vietnam has done a lot of weird things to the world. The Chinese are over here studying with the Northern Ontario Ministry of Natural Resources because the Ontario MNR are the best fire fighters in the world and they will tell you so. So while we were hovering and levitating over the torching spruce, it hit me that this is what Moses saw, and it's no symbol. One is in The Presence of the Flame. Different kinds of energy take place in different parts of the world. Up here it's fire. There have always been fires up here. That's how the boreal forest remakes itself: the spruce cones can't open up and generate seeds until they've been through a forest fire. They're too hard, they have to be burnt open. That's how it works. Maybe that's how we work. I saw what I saw; I guess I was meant to go up that day in that helicopter and see this towering sucker torch right in front of my eyes.

Watch this!

Watch this happen!

It's a matter of getting your eye behind it, and focusing, and just keeping on watching, and not freaking, or falling out.

This is the fire season up here in Sioux Lookout. Q

The old man stepped
into the crowd for
protection